PREACHING THE GOSPEL
Without Easy Answers

PREACHING THE GOSPEL
Without Easy Answers

ROBERT CUMMINGS NEVILLE

ABINGDON PRESS / *Nashville*

PREACHING THE GOSPEL WITHOUT EASY ANSWERS

Copyright © 2005 by Abingdon Press

This book is printed on acid-free paper.

Library of Congress Cataloging-in-Publication Data

Neville, Robert C.
   Preaching the Gospel without easy answers / Robert Cummings Neville.
      p. cm.
   Includes bibliographical references.
   ISBN 0-687-33176-5 (bindng: pbk. : alk. paper)
   1. Preaching. I. Title.

   BV4211.3.N48 2005
   252'.076--dc22

3-1-08

2005026475

All scripture quotations unless noted otherwise are taken from the New Revised Standard Version of the Bible, copyright 1989, Division of Christian Education of the National Council of the Churches of Christ in the United States of America. Used by permission. All rights reserved.

Scripture quotations noted KJV are from the King James or Authorized Version of the Bible.

"Stand By Me" by Charles Albert Tindley, ca. 1906.

"It Is Well with My Soul." Words by Horatio G. Spafford, 1873.

"Are Ye Able." Words by Earl Marlatt. 1926.

Lections from Revised Common Lectionary copyright © 1992 by the Consultation on Common Texts (CCT), 1275 K Street NW, Suite 202, Washington, DC 20005-4097. All rights reserved.

"On Marriage" was previously published in part in *Zion's Herald* (January-February 2004). Reprinted with permission.

05 06 07 08 09 10 11 12 13 14—10 9 8 7 6 5 4 3 2 1

MANUFACTURED IN THE UNITED STATES OF AMERICA

*For the Actual and Virtual Congregations of
Marsh Chapel 2003–2004*

CONTENTS

PREFACE

TOO OFTEN PREACHERS believe they should talk down to their hearers. Having been told that it does not matter what they say if they cannot first communicate it, they struggle to be understood by everyone, even those least prepared to think the Word of God with them. Well, no preacher goes that far, actually. But every preacher feels, and many cater to, the tension between saying things simply enough not to be misunderstood and struggling for the language complex enough to state the gospel contained in the text as made relevant for the affairs at hand. Like politicians, many preachers gravitate to sound bites that are already in their people's cultural vocabulary. The result can be dumbed-down preaching that tells people what they already know, and already know to be too simple.

The expectation in a university church—in my case Marsh Chapel at Boston University—is that the hardest problems will be addressed with the most sophisticated kind of inquiry available and with the most imaginative apparatus for translating the gospel from the Bible into life. The congregation also expects the preacher to deal with the most urgent religious issues of the day, which included the debate about gay marriage in Massachusetts during the year when I delivered these sermons. What congregation would want less demanding preaching? What congregation would want deliberately oversimplified interpretations of the Word of God or evasions of the religious issues that fill the news? Some congregations might complain about having to think hard, and some might bristle at the preacher's stand on the urgent issues. But not a one would want to be patronized or led away from relevant thinking. The university church is just like other congregations in this regard.

Marsh Chapel serves two roles at Boston University. On the one hand, it is the center of the university chaplaincy that serves students and university community members of many religions and faiths. Under my title as Chaplain of the University, I support and, where necessary, coordinate the various agencies that address the religious needs of Jews, Muslims, Buddhists, Daoists, Confucians, Hindus, and many smaller faith communities, as well as Christians of many varieties. On the other hand, Marsh Chapel is the center for the support and worship life of the interdenominational Protestant university congregation whose pastor I am, as Dean of Marsh Chapel.

The interdenominational Protestant congregation that worships on Sunday mornings is actually three connected congregations. One is a core of people who stay with us all year, year after year, treating Marsh Chapel as their church home. This core contains university faculty and staff as well as people from the larger community, young people and old, men and women, native-born Americans and people from many countries, races, and cultures across the globe. The core congregation stays for coffee after church and puts on a wonderful monthly potluck lunch. The second related congregation is made up of students who attend during their university years and usually only during the academic year. Moreover, their participation varies with the vicissitudes of the academic year. We have a marvelous Chapel Choir, most of whose members are students and whose participation is very regular. Students are served by many programs throughout the week during the academic year, in addition to Sunday morning worship. The third congregation is the radio audience that participates "virtually" through the regular live broadcast of our Sunday services on the university's National Public Radio station, WBUR, which is also available live through Internet connections. The letters, calls, and e-mail communications we receive about these broadcasts indicate a vastly varied virtual congregation, including many who, for reasons of principle, would not attend a Christian service. But they listen, many of them very faithfully, because of their expectations of preaching from a university pulpit. (Perhaps the most astute ones listen for the music instead.) The sermons here all come from the 2003-04 academic year, ending with the summer before the beginning of the 2004-05 academic year. The sermon "On Marriage" was previously published with slight modifications in *Zion's Herald*. For the most part, the texts for the sermons have been drawn from the Revised Common Lectionary and, when cited, use the New Revised Standard Version translation. Nearly always, the sermons deal closely with the texts, developing scriptural images even when not citing them directly. Therefore it helps to read the texts in advance of the sermons, although many readers will be familiar with them anyway.

The complexity of preaching today requires sermons of many genres. Some here are plainly theological, others more spiritual, some political, and several of them occasional, dictated by special circumstances. All of them are intended to be pastoral, responding to some pastoral need or other. I have deleted lines from sermons that deal with many of the particularities of the congregation that would not be of interest to a larger audience. But the references to current events, especially those of the Boston Red Sox, remain. I apologize to Yankee fans for citing the prayers of the Red Sox hopefuls who were rewarded in the fall following this series of sermons by four victories over New York after being three down in the pennant play-off, and by four more straight victories over the St. Louis Cardinals in the World Series, winning for the first time in eighty-six years. If it weren't for the idolatry involved, what better parable could there be for faith than that of the Red Sox fans?

I have made no attempt to disguise the fact these sermons are preached in a university church that is responsive to the academic as well as liturgical calendar. The reference in the Easter Vigil sermon to the "Romans" above our congregation—in the undercroft of the chapel—refers to the fact that our Roman Catholic brothers and sisters conduct a glorious Easter Vigil in the main sanctuary while our smaller Protestant congregation worships below.

More than anything, these sermons are shaped by how abashed I am at the wildness of God, the divine immensity, the abyss of God's creative fire. In the face of this divine mystery, we stand under unconditional judgment with no excuses for our willful ignorance, spiritual torpor, moral perversity, or collective self-deceptions. At the same time the saving grace of God can transform and sanctify all that, blowing wildly from the strangest directions and stirring up the spirit in all those tiny dead places. Without appealing to any fancy miracles of divine action, my testimony, in the Wesleyan tradition, is to the intimate might of the wild God, manifest most clearly in Jesus Christ, to bring about new life in ultimate perspective.

FOUNDATIONS

1.

WHAT TO TRUST

Jeremiah 17:5-10
1 Corinthians 15:12-20
Luke 6:17-26*

EW OCCASIONS EXIST in which it is a comfort to read Jeremiah. He was the ultimate complainer, though he had good company with most of the other prophets. He gave his name to the fire-and-brimstone sermons of early American history that we call "Jeremiads." Nevertheless, today Jeremiah brings a word of comfort. For we live in a time of great wild forces over which we have little control, and we need something to trust. Once upon a time, people could trust their families to keep them safe and economically supplied. For most of us, that is no more. In some poor countries such as Rwanda, even having a family sets you up to lose in clan warfare. Americans put great trust in education as an institution that trains and increases the power that individuals and communities might have. Yet in most American cities, the educational institutions are so unequal that the rich get farther ahead and so many of the poor just drop off the charts. Americans have trusted the federal government to support the poor during times of economic hardship, to protect the environment from destruction by greedy exploitation, to protect us from the ravages of war, especially unnecessary war, and to protect our honor among nations. Yet on all these fronts things are getting worse fast. Americans have trusted themselves individually, with a fierce pioneering independence, and yet as Jeremiah said, the human heart is perverse. In sum, Jeremiah said, "Cursed are those who trust in mere mortals." Jeremiah's solution, of course, is that we should trust in God.

Psalm 62 says: "For God alone my soul waits in silence; from him comes my salvation. God alone is my rock and my salvation, my fortress; I shall never

---

* Lections for the Sixth Sunday after the Epiphany, Year C.

be shaken." Surely it is good Christian piety, Jewish and Muslim piety, too, for that matter, to trust only in God, knowing that human institutions and individuals are not trustworthy. Yet when we back away from the piety of this sentiment, the picture is not clear. Two items of unclarity are mixed together: how do we imagine the God in whom we should trust, and just what trust is about.

I use the verb "imagine" advisedly, because we think of such things as the God in whom we trust in terms of images. The Bible and the Christian traditions have many images of God. I have spoken about Isaiah's vision of God as a huge man set on a kingly throne, the hem of whose robe filled the Temple, a very anthropomorphic image, like that of God the warrior who leads Israel out of Egypt. Some Christians imagine God as a kinder, gentler version of the Grand Old Man in the Sky, while others continue with Isaiah to imagine God as a judgmental king.

Counter-images of God in the Bible seem to be deliberate deconstructions of the anthropomorphic images. For instance, when God descends on Mount Sinai to deliver the commandments to Moses, the finite environment almost breaks apart, not being able to contain the Holy One of Israel. The mountain shakes violently and a sound as of mighty trumpets rises and rises and rises. The foot of the mountain is roped off so people will not come close and be destroyed.

Then there are images of God as Creator of the entire world, higher than the distinction between light and dark, form and chaos. John goes so far as to say that God is love, not a being who loves but love itself. The early Christian theologians quickly noted that God as Creator transcends any distinctions, creates time and space, and is not to be represented in images or concepts except through symbols that don't quite apply. The author of Colossians, for instance, says that Jesus Christ, the incarnate Logos, is the first visible image of the invisible, that is unimaginable, God.

Without being frivolous, let me characterize this spectrum of images in the following way. Toward the anthropomorphic end of the spectrum, we have a small God who can play roles as a finite character in the story of Israel, or in our own stories. Toward the transcendent end, we have an immense God, where "immense" means not only very large but immeasurably so. "Immense" means not-measurable, hence not describable except in carefully controlled symbols. The Christian theological tradition by and large, and rightly to my mind, has said that the real God is the immense one, not the small one. The images of the anthropomorphic God are mere metaphors, and we should be very careful with them, however important they are in many areas of religious life. The images of the immense God are serious efforts to grapple with a profound mystery.

The meaning of "trust" in God is obviously correlated with the spectrum of images of God. When we imagine God in anthropomorphic ways, thinking of God as an agent separate from us, within time and space, and interacting with the rest of the world, playing roles in our histories and lives, trust means expecting God to do things for us. Sometimes we imagine God to behave like a righteous king governing history, rewarding the good and punishing the evil, with a little mercy thrown in for the penitent. The Bible tells the story of God covenanting with Israel. Other times we imagine God to be interacting with us like another person, responding to prayers like a good big person would. The news about these images of the small God is very bad, I fear. The good people are not always rewarded, and the evil are not always punished. God's promises to Israel as the chosen people, interpreted in strictly historical terms, have not been fulfilled—quite the opposite. David's dynasty has not been kept intact. Jesus did not return in the time-frame the Bible laid down. Good people, even innocent children, sicken, suffer, and die, despite our deepest prayers. However much parts of the Bible suggest that some finite God runs the universe like a righteous kingdom, that is empirically false, and other parts of the Bible admit that. We cannot trust some small God to make us secure, to reward moral behavior, or to control history according to some preconceived and promised plan. Instead we ourselves need to work directly to make our own families, institutions, governments, personal characters, and skills trustworthy. However faulty they are now, they can be improved. This is our public and personal moral responsibility. And we cannot hope for more in the management of life as it is played out in time. If our only images are of a small God, trust is vain, and the only realistic course is practical atheism.

Trust in the immense God is a different matter. Here we relate to the eternal Creator of space, time, and history, the Creator of all things that can be conceived to act within the historical cosmos. The question of trust in the immense God is not about safety or success as measured by the temporal unfolding of our lives, by "the world," as the New Testament calls it. Trust is about whether we are sustained so as to be fulfilled in relation to the immense God. Here is the very heart of the Christian gospel. Within time, we should expect troubles and crosses, as well as such benefits and satisfactions as we can secure by luck and our own limited means. Within the eternity relating us to the immense God, we are resurrected to a richer sense of life than temporal life affords. The cross and resurrection are the defining themes of the Christian Way. As we approach Lent and Easter, we shall ponder these themes often.

What does it mean to trust the immense God? It means that God's eternal creativity within which we already and always live, move, and have our being gives us the power to live rightly and in fulfillment before God. Nothing in the world can prevent that if we trust that creativity and use the power.

To live rightly before God requires living justly: we always have the power to seek justice and commit our substance to it, even if justice cannot be achieved fully and every apparently just pattern also has its injustices. The world can prevent success, but it cannot destroy our search for and commitment to justice, which is righteousness.

To live rightly before God requires living with pious deference to every creature, appreciating its value regardless of how it might be reduced to merely instrumental value for human life: our ecological environments, our clans, and our primitive passions are all due the piety of deference even when we order them for higher purposes. The world cannot destroy our piety, though it is easily lost through our own thoughtlessness.

To live rightly before God requires living with the faith that our own situation can be engaged with courage, no matter how painful, frustrating, ephemeral, and distasteful. We do not have to pretend to be rich, beautiful, and in Shangri-La, nor to complain about being poor, bald, and cold in whatever place we live. The world cannot destroy our faith to engage our actual lives; it can only make them vain by worldly standards.

To live rightly before God requires organizing our lives with the hope that we can achieve something of value ultimately considered, something that makes a contribution to the divine life. The world might frustrate our hope to achieve what we want, but it cannot deny us the hope itself and its organizational power for our lives.

Righteousness, piety, faith, and hope are the virtues for living before God, and together they add up to something more, however fulfilling they are on their own: they add up to love. Love seeks the best for its object, appreciates its object for its own value, engages the object with full devotion, and organizes itself so as to live with its object in a way that enhances the good of all. Any love that lacks such righteousness, pious appreciation, faithful engagement, or directing hope is deficient in obvious ways. No matter how poor and incompetent we are, by our very created existence we can live with righteousness in pursuit of justice, with piety in deference to the worth in each thing, with faith in our situation, with hope to live before God well, and with love in the image of God. The world cannot take these away.

Whom do we love? God and our neighbors, of course, and the whole created realm. The particular shape of loving neighbors comes from just who your neighbors are, especially those who are your enemies. There is no such thing as righteousness in general, only justice for these people, no piety in general, only deference to these things, no faith in general, only engagement with your situations, no hope in general, only your path with these pilgrims. Love is of the particulars.

God is the greatest particular, the singular Creator of this crazy universe, who gives you your sunsets and flowers, your songs and dances, your successes and failures, your odd friends, your resolute enemies, your pains, your ills, and your death. God, your vastly fecund Creator, gives you your life, threaded with others through a cloth of only unique strands bearing all risings and ceasings, all starts and stops, all joys and pains, all births and deaths. The immense God is not some small deity dedicated to doing only nice things. Loving the singular Creator of your existence is hard. Loving your enemies is necessary practice for loving the God of Immensity, because whereas your enemies only *might* kill you, God surely will in the end.

To be a lover, loving our God, loving the persons, friends, and enemies of our neighborhood, and loving the whole of creation that we can know, is to be in concord and consent with God's own act as Creator. To love is to be in harmony with God, the completion and fulfillment of the divine creative act, and it is to add a harmony lacking when love fails. The whole of Christian discipline and practice is aimed to create communities and individuals that image God as creative lover. God gives us the power to love in the gift of our creation itself: no matter how much we suffer and lose by worldly standards, we always can love. That God creates us with the power to love no matter what is what we can trust for the good of our very being, despite all the troubles of the world that crucify us.

One final thought. When we do trust the God of Immensity and move on toward perfection in love, then the knots and tangles of our fights with life fall away and the powers of divine fecundity move through us like music. We move with the flow of creation rather than against it and have more patience for righteousness, more perception for piety, more courage for faith, more energy for hope, and more wild passion for love. Although our lives will still be filled with troubles as well as joys and have many dry times, trusting God we shall not be like "a shrub in the desert" or "live in the parched places of the wilderness, in an uninhabited salt land." We "shall be like a tree planted by water, sending out its roots by the stream. It shall not fear when heat comes, and its leaves shall stay green; in the year of drought it is not anxious, and it does not cease to bear fruit." Trust our immense God and eternal home, and despite everything you will have abundant life here and now. Amen.

2.

CHRIST THE IMAGE OF THE INVISIBLE GOD

Colossians 1:15-28
Luke 10:38-42*

W E CHRISTIANS RELATE to God by relating to Jesus Christ. Of course, Christians share many things with people of other religions, for instance a commitment to ethical life, a love of justice and peace, a reverence for holy people and places, and awe at the majesty of what is most ultimate, known as God in the language of monotheisms but going by other names in other religions. What makes Christians different, and what distinctly shapes our approach to ethics, justice and peace, reverence, and awe, is our relation to Jesus Christ. According to St. Paul, Christians are supposed to be "in Christ," although he had difficulty saying what that meant.

Our two texts today present very different images of Jesus Christ. The Gospel from Luke shows Jesus as a teacher in the intimate setting of a dinner party. Other texts from Luke present various other settings for Jesus as the herald of the kingdom of God and the healer. One text shows Jesus talking with a lawyer about eternal life, with Jesus telling the story of the good Samaritan. Our text today is set in the home of Mary and Martha. We know them much more fully from the Gospel of John in which they are shown as having a long and intimate friendship with Jesus. They were a well-to-do family in Bethany, near Jerusalem, where Jesus spent a lot of time. John tells of Jesus raising their brother Lazarus from the dead, which was both Jesus' most important miracle, according to John, and also the reason why the authorities became concerned about Jesus and resolved to

---

* Lections for Proper 11, Sunday between July 17 and July 23, Year C.

9

put him to death. The household of Mary and Martha was very important for Jesus.

The incident in our text contrasts their characters in ways that have become almost clichés in Christian preaching: Mary is spiritual while Martha is practical. It was Martha who issued the dinner invitation and prepared the banquet, while Mary sat at Jesus' feet as a disciple. You doubtless have heard sermons about these two personality types for Christian women, the pillar of the church who cooks the meals and the devotee who reads spiritual books all day. Both are approved, although Jesus was a bit annoyed that Martha was making such a fuss, possibly because she wanted more attention. She also seemed a bit jealous of the attention Mary was getting as a "Jesus-freak." Jesus' response was to say that one dish would be plenty for the dinner and that she did not have to serve up a banquet.

What is important about this story is not anything that Jesus was teaching; his remarks are not recorded, although Luke does quote Jesus' teachings in many other passages. What is important is his personality, the way he handled the touchy relations between the sisters. He had great affection for them both and was able to give Martha credit as his senior hostess and cook while also saying that she did not have to work so hard. He did not say that doe-eyed discipleship is more important than hospitality, only that hospitality can be kept in due proportion. He comforted Martha about her excessive worries and distractions. This is not Jesus the charismatic teacher or magical healer. This is Jesus the very human and hungry friend who adjusts and perfects the way people around him exercise love.

Compare this presentation of Jesus—it's not even fitting to attach the title "Christ" to him in this vignette—with the text from Colossians. Colossians is what theologians call "high Christology," focusing on the divinity of Christ. Our passage does not use the personal name "Jesus," although Colossians elsewhere uses the phrase "Christ Jesus." The first thing our passage does is to call attention to the distinction between the invisible God and Christ as God's image. "Invisible" as applied to God in the first century does not mean only that God cannot be seen because of being an immaterial spirit. It means rather that God is so high above human comprehension and categories that nothing can describe God directly. John says (1:18) that no one has ever seen God, which is a change from claims in Exodus that Moses and others saw God. By Jesus' time, people understood God as so high as to be the Creator of everything that can be imagined. As our Colossians text puts it, God created all things visible *and* invisible in the sense of being spiritual and therefore is above them. To say that Christ is the image of this High God is to say that he is the first thing that can be known and described about the unimaginable God. Paul, in 2 Corinthians 4, and the author of Hebrews, in the first chapter, also say that Christ is the image of God in this sense.

Colossians says that Christ provides an image by which we can grasp the unimaginable God, because Christ is the firstborn of all creation. Christ is the first creature who then becomes the means by which all other creatures come to be. "[F]or in him all things in heaven and on earth were created, things visible and invisible, whether thrones or dominions or rulers or powers." "Thrones, dominions, rulers, and powers" are various ranks of angels, invisible spirits, according to the first-century belief. The idea of Christ as the one who is "before all things" and in whom "all things hold together" is like the idea of Logos at the beginning of the Gospel of John, a primordial structure and power by means of which all the world is created. In John, the suggestion is that the Logos is a companion to God the Creator. Colossians is plain that Christ is the first creature, subordinate to God yet prior to all else.

Later theologians in Western Christianity would side with John, interpreting him to mean that the Logos is equal to God and is fully a part of Trinitarian divinity. Theologians in Eastern Orthodox Christianity would keep the emphasis on subordination in Colossians, emphasizing that the Son is begotten by the Father and that this is not a reciprocal relation. However we line up with that later dispute, Colossians says that we understand the incomprehensible God by understanding Christ.

What is it that we understand of Christ? First, as mentioned, Christ is the structure through which all other things are created. Second, Colossians says that Christ is the head of the church and likens the church to the body of Christ. Because the church is supposed to be the body that properly worships God, Christ is the Head that directs that worship: we should worship God as Christ says to worship and conduct ourselves ethically in God's kingdom according to the model of Christ our Head. Third, Colossians says that Christ is not only the firstborn of all creation but also the firstborn of the dead, the first to be raised. Here the text is clearly talking about Christ Jesus, the man, whom the Christians knew to have been crucified and raised from the dead. Thus, as image of God, we understand Christ Jesus to reveal God as not only Creator but also as Redeemer. "For in him all the fullness of God was pleased to dwell," which is to say that everything divine that can fit into a human being fit into Jesus, and by relating to the person of Jesus we find the redeeming Creator.

Now I know this high Christology is complicated, working with symbols that seem strange and unintelligible in our culture. But please bear with the argument in Colossians for a few more minutes. The text characterizes the ordinary state of human beings as estranged from God and hostile in mind: this is the human predicament from which salvation must rescue us. We are estranged and hostile. God reconciles us to himself, says Colossians, "by making peace through the blood of [Christ's] cross." The reference here is to the institution of ritual sacrifice in Israelite religion. According to Leviticus as well as Exodus, Numbers, and Deuteronomy, Israel was a holy nation that could present itself blameless and irreproachable to God as long as it kept the covenant. But when the covenant was broken in any way, large or small, the people had to sacrifice something to God, grain or an animal, in order to repair their holiness and ability to approach God. God in the Torah instituted the sacrifice rituals as means to repair the covenant because God knew the covenant would be impossible for people. God's mercy provided a ready remedy.

Christians interpreted human sin as so great as not to be reparable by any sacrifice of grain or animals. So just as God had earlier provided the rituals for sacrificial repair of the covenant, now God provides Christ the firstborn of all creation as himself the sacrifice that once again reconciles human beings to God.

The idea that a sacrifice can reconcile estranged and hostile parties is uncomfortable to modern sensibilities. We are very far from the Levitical sensibilities of the ancient world. Yet we do understand something of Colossians' argument: it was human beings who were estranged from and hostile to God—God was not estranged and hostile, according to our text. So God sent that which is most precious, the firstborn of creation, as a sacrifice to call us back from estrangement and hostility, and that in the form of the man Jesus who had to be crucified. Because of that sacrifice we have a fresh start, and never again does the sacrifice have to be made no matter what evil we do.

You might ask how we can tolerate these images of blood sacrifice. They were commonplace for first-century Christians but are gross for us. Yet there is something in human evil, something in the evil of natural suffering and the deep injustice of the institutions on which we have built our society that is even more gross. The blood guilt we bear for what it costs the earth for us to live, for the harm we do one another, for the repressions built into civilization even at its best, calls for blood sacrifice. This is only a symbol, a symbol used by the early Christians to understand the crucifixion of Jesus. But we cannot do with a less powerful symbol. Christ the symbol of God reveals God as the Creator whose love accepts blood guilt and reconciles us even when we are estranged and hostile. That symbol cleanses our hearts and directs our faith even when we cannot take it literally.

The practical question for contemporary Christians is how we can relate to Jesus Christ whose blood bought us redemption, knowing how alien these symbols are. I believe we need to understand first that wise and loving Jesus who traveled about teaching that we always live in the sight of God, that we are in God's kingdom whether we know it or not, and that what counts in God's kingdom is our practice of love. The teaching is important, but the person who taught it is more important to know, the friend so kind as to straighten out Martha and Mary. The Bible gives us much to work around in our imagination as we think about this Jesus who would be our friend too. Can we imagine Jesus gently correcting our faults as he did Martha's? To be related to Jesus as his friend, and to him as our friend, is the first step in relation.

The second is to see God in Jesus, who is his primary image. God is humble, like Jesus, condescending to heal our little estrangements and hostilities as Jesus healed Martha's. Yet the savagery of nature's indifference to suffering, the outrage of death, the depths of greed, and the perverse human pleasure in causing pain constitute an evil strain in creation so profound that a simple teacher's love cannot heal it. We need to symbolize the extremity of God's love with the savagery of the crucifixion's blood sacrifice if we are to recognize what needs healing. So it is Christ Jesus crucified that lets us engage the High God whose redeeming power is equal to creation's need. And it is Christ Jesus the firstborn of the dead who leads us to live before God as redeemed and renewed persons.

Only through such powerful symbols can we admit the problem and embrace the cosmic power of the answer. These symbols allow us to engage the problem honestly and to engage God as imaged by Christ Jesus. Even if the symbol of blood sacrifice cannot be tolerated as a literal explanation of redemptive history, only that image can engage us with the unimaginable God so that we see the seriousness of creation's redemption of which we are a part. Only when we live in Christ Jesus, firstborn of all creation and friend of Mary and Martha, can we let God's cosmic love seep into our bones and sinews to heal estrangement and hostility and finally make us lovers. Only then can we envision the invisible God in the person of Christ Jesus, our lover and beloved, pioneer of our faith. We are grateful for people who can accept these symbols naively. We praise God that we can see the symbols broken and yet also live by them to engage our Creator and Redeemer. Amen.

3.

DEEDS OF POWER

Esther 7:1-6, 9-10; 9:20-22
James 5:13-20
*Mark 9:38-50**

HAVE YOU EVER longed for miracles, for what Jesus called deeds of power? They come in many kinds, not even counting prayers for the Red Sox or pleas to find a parking place. Consider the story of Esther, Queen of Persia. She was not an aristocrat, merely a beautiful woman in the harem of King Ahasuerus (also known as Xerxes) who was made queen because of her sexual charms and docility. She was a Jew, and the Jews were hated by a high Persian official named Haman who was a member of the House of Agag. Agag had been killed by the Israelite prophet Samuel, as you can read in 1 Samuel 15, and most of his people were slaughtered by King Saul. Haman plotted to destroy all the Jews who lived in Persian dominions and enrich himself. Esther found out about this and manipulated events so the King punished Haman instead and put her own kinsman, Mordecai, into a position of great power, thus saving the Jews. This salvation of the entire Jewish community is commemorated in the festival of Purim that Jewish people celebrate to this day.

Would it not be a great miracle, a deed of power, if some world leader arose from obscurity to do just the right thing to turn aside the warring madness that engulfs our world? There must be some way to vent the hatred all around and to let the rich nations see their duty to be just to the poor. In the past, great leaders sometimes have arisen in times of crisis— think of Abraham Lincoln and Martin Luther King Jr. They were miracles in a very important sense, and they are rare. The international political world today needs a miracle. A great peacemaking leader would be a

---

* Lections for Proper 21, Sunday between September 25 and October 1, Year B.

miracle because the odds are so great against such a person arising and having an opportunity like Esther's to make a significant difference. Although the Jews were delivered in Persia, they were not delivered in the Holocaust, at least not enough of them and not early enough. Deeds of power are miraculous because they usually do not happen. Nothing in the Esther story, by the way, suggests that God had anything to do with the miracle.

Jesus' own use of the phrase "deed of power" in Mark 9:39 is in reference to an anonymous exorcist who was casting out demons in Jesus' name. Whatever you think of ancient exorcism, it was a power widely believed to be exercised by many people, not only by Jesus or his disciples. Exorcism was not a matter of praying that God would work a miracle but rather a power inherent in the exorcist or the "patient," something Jesus explained as deriving from faith in God. The disciples were upset that this anonymous exorcist was so successful when he was not actually a member of Jesus' own following. Jesus, however, remarked that "whoever is not against us is for us." Given the fact that Jesus' own disciples had spotty records as exorcists, he was probably glad to get the outsider's help.

Don't we long for the surprise outsider miracle? We work so hard to cope with life's troubles, many of which can be rightly described as demonic, and yet our efforts are not deeds of power. Then someone unexpected and not of our community comes along and does just the right thing. Who would have thought that the civil rights struggle in the United States could be transformed into deeds of power by Martin Luther King Jr. studying Gandhi's philosophy of aggressive nonviolence? The situation in India in his time was different from that in King's America. Gandhi was not a Christian. Gandhi was Hindu, yet his deeds of power in India sparked deeds of power here. How unexpected and rare! It was a miracle in its strange way.

Or consider the community James addressed in his letter. His community struggled to be faithful to doctrine as James urged them that "correct" faith is not enough: they need to practice their faith. In today's text, James addresses very practical matters. If you are suffering, pray. If you are joyful, sing. If someone is sick, bring the elders of the community to pray over them, anointing them with oil, for "the prayer of faith will save the sick." Confess sins to one another, and they will be forgiven. If someone brings back a member of the community who has wandered from the truth, the one who brings that person back will have a multitude of sins covered. "The prayer of the righteous is powerful and effective," said James.

Now we all know, as James's community must have known, that not everyone who wanders is brought back. Not every sin confessed with the mouth is confessed with the heart. And not every sick person who is prayed over gets well. My wife and I know that from experience. We had a daughter who developed heart disease as an infant. We prayed and prayed. She was operated on and we prayed and prayed, as did our congregation, St. Stephen's Methodist Church in the Bronx. Our daughter died six days after surgery. All that praying did not avail to accomplish our heart's desire. A miracle was there nonetheless. At the time of our deepest, most raw, soul-numbing grief, my wife and I were conscious of the prayers and support of the congregation and were thankful. Yet that wasn't the half of it. When our daughter was baptized, the entire congregation had stood up in joy as her godparents. When she died a few months later, I believe the entire congregation took off work to attend the funeral. Our daughter was conceived in the life of that congregation, cheered by them at her birth, received into the Christian life in the arms of all the members, and was returned to God with universal tears and hallelujahs. That was a miracle. Her life and death in that congregation were fully powered by the Holy Spirit, a deed of power embracing her, the congregation, and us. What a privilege and grace her short life was! I served as associate at St. Stephen's another dozen years and don't know whether it ever again was so God-filled. Nor have my family and I ever found a congregation that carried Christ and us together so well since. But because of that miracle of our daughter's life and death in that congregation, with all the songs of joy, prayers through suffering, and tears of good-bye, I know what Christ's people can be. I've seen the love. I've felt the faith. My hope does not shake, even when I wade through the Christian klutziness that has discouraged so many of you. There! You have my testimony that I have witnessed the church as miracle.

How do we understand these deeds of power? To think of them as interventions of an anthropomorphic God who is persuaded by our prayers or needs is a mistake. The evidence is all to the contrary concerning either our persuasiveness or God's consistency and good will relative to our heart's desires. That conception of God as a magical person is simply too small. Rather these deeds of power should be understood as grace.

Grace is the power of God to make good things. Ordinarily we let the goodness of God's whole creation sink into the background of our consciousness as we focus attention on some particular good we would like to have. Most of us worry about seemingly inevitable conflicts in world affairs, with no end in sight. So we would like the grace of a miracle of peacemaking leadership, forgetting to be grateful for the grace of having cultures worth fighting for. We desperately want our loved ones to be well and safe, forgetting to be grateful for the grace of having lives with loved ones in them. We pray for the miracle of an A on an exam, forgetting to be grateful for the grace of getting an education. We long for the miraculous break for our career, forgetting to be grateful for a society in which careers are possible. Human attention just has this feature that it focuses on some things by putting other things in the background. If we focus on the miracles we specifically long for, we forget the countless deeds of power in the gracious creations that surround us. And when we fail to get what we long for, our disappointment, perhaps even grief, can blind us to the rest of life that is so full of grace.

So let us recall and contemplate the graces that surround us, God's creation of good things for which we should be grateful.

God the Father creates a world whose every part is a wondrous harmony of form and power, uniqueness and relation, assembly and dissolution. The singular swirl of cosmic gases is grace. The clumping of galaxies is grace. The earth is grace. Its hospitality to human life is grace. The earth's crust is grace. Its water is grace. Its atmosphere is grace. The earth is a garden world and that's grace. People have families, that's grace. Cultures are grace. The arts are grace. Tilling the soil is grace. Building cities is grace. Flying off-planet is grace. Insects are grace. Birds are grace. Pets are grace. Laughter is grace. Crying is grace. Feeling so as to laugh and cry is grace. Gain is grace. Loss is grace. Birth is grace. Growth is grace. Learning is grace. Work is grace. Aging is grace. Death is grace. Wisdom is grace. Confusion is grace. Beauty is grace. Life is grace. "God saw everything that he had made, and indeed, it was very good. And there was evening and there was morning, the sixth day" (Gen. 1:31).

Despite the cosmos filled with grace, we have not consistently responded with gratitude, the natural response to grace. Instead we have complained because the grace was not where we wanted it to be. We complain there is no peace when we will to hold onto control. We complain that our loved ones die when there are others to love. We complain that others have the luck when we don't take responsibility. And deep down we feel guilty for the price that our own civilized existence exacts from the environment, from others, and from our own freedom. With guilts and complaints, we turn from the Creator, ashamed, gratitude curdles to bitterness, and we forget the cosmos of grace.

Grace upon grace, Jesus came saying, "Wake up! The kingdom is at hand. Not your world of petty deeds of power but the cosmos of grace." Jesus said, Blessed are the humble, not the power brokers, and that is grace. Jesus said our sins are forgiven, and that is grace. Jesus said that mercy is divine, and that is grace. Jesus said God loves us, and that is grace. Jesus said to love one another, and that is grace. Jesus loved his friends and made them love others, and that is grace. Jesus' friends loved others and made them love others, and that is grace. Those others in the name of Jesus love us and make us love others, and that is grace. Jesus nails our guilts to the cross and that is grace. Jesus turns our bitter complaints to songs of joy, and that is grace. Jesus redeems us from evil lives, and that is grace. Jesus draws us to a cosmic kingdom filled with grace, and that is grace. Jesus shows us God, and that is grace. Jesus is our friend, and that is grace. We flee from God but, meeting Jesus, God is where we flee, and that is grace.

So how then do we live as created, fallen, and redeemed people? The Holy Spirit fills life with deeds of power for sanctification. To pray our heart's desire in things great and small brings grace. To sing and pray in the congregation of God's people brings grace. To study Jesus brings grace. To live together as friends among Jesus' friends brings grace. To spend ourselves for the poor brings grace. To risk ourselves for justice brings grace. To build homes brings grace. To serve communities brings grace. To play brings grace. To run brings grace. To think brings grace. To touch God's creatures in all their gracious loveliness brings grace, even when the touch bears harm and finally wears us out. To bless the Lord who gives and takes away brings grace. The holiness of the redeemed life is to love God and all God's creatures. We have the grace for that.

So I invite you to open your eyes to the deeds of power all around us. If you have troubles, cry to God with all your heart. But remember that your heart is also full of peace and joy because of the overflowing abundance of grace in our lives. If you don't think your heart is full of peace and joy because it feels like confusion and despair, look deeper. For the depths of the heart open onto God and the world to be loved. What a grace that is! Praise the Father who creates a world of grace, praise the Son who is the grace of salvation, and praise the Holy Spirit in whose grace we live by the love of God. Amen.

4.

TO TURN THINGS UPSIDE DOWN (AN ADVENT SERMON)

Micah 5:2-5a
Luke 1:47-55
Hebrews 10:5-10
*Luke 1:39-45**

THE STORIES OF Jesus' birth in the Gospels of Matthew and Luke are great treasures of the human heritage, significant far beyond the community of people who accept Jesus as the Christ. Most of those stories, in one way or another, express two of the great themes of the Christian religion. The first is that God is the gracious Giver of good gifts. This theme can be understood by children. We Americans have turned Christmas into a children's holiday, focusing on the baby Jesus as a gift to the world, responding with a celebration of gifts to Jesus and gifts to our own children and to one another. Now is not the time to complain about the materialism and consumerism of the American Christmas—time enough for that later. Now we should simply rejoice in the practice of giving gifts to others, one of the very best senses in which human beings can embody the image of God. We rejoice also in the practice of gratitude for gifts received, which is the essence of piety. God's gifts, of course, are cosmic: God creates the world; God shapes its evolution to provide a habitat for human beings; God gives us consciousness, reason, and freedom; God redeems us when we fall; and God gives us a home in eternity. The sum

---

* Lections for the Fourth Sunday of Advent, Year C.

21

of our gratitude for all these things is to become lovers and givers like God. Children get a foretaste of this heavy-duty Christian metaphysics in the gift-giving of Christmas.

The second great theme of the Christmas stories is not easily accessible to children. It is that God's gifts turn upside down the customary expectations of the world, especially those about power, authority, and righteousness. The core of Mary's song, called the Magnificat, says God "has scattered the proud in the thoughts of their hearts. He has brought down the powerful from their thrones, and lifted up the lowly; he has filled the hungry with good things, and sent the rich away empty." God gave a child to Mary's cousin Elizabeth when she was far too old to conceive, and the angel Gabriel remarked that "nothing will be impossible with God." Jesus was the heir of David, but he was born in a stable because there was no room at the inn. The wise men brought riches, not for King Herod who wanted their obeisance, but for the baby in the stable. Who remembers Herod the Great now except as a villain in Jesus' story? God turns human expectations upside down, and history is filled with divine irony.

We Americans are living through a crisis of expectations turned upside down, and it causes great confusion. Our sense of national identity, of the values that make us Americans, is grounded in the mythos of our origins. The real history is more complex than the mythos, and yet the mythos is the source of our commitments to justice and national integrity. Have we been turned upside down and forgotten our origins? Have we Americans forgotten the covenant of our youth as a nation, the gratitude to God for our love of freedom and self-determination, of brotherhood and justice for all? Have we forgotten that the founders of New England sought the land here to be free, free especially to practice their religion, because they were not free to do so in England? Have we forgotten that the colonists fought a bloody war of independence from England because England disregarded that freedom and tried to enforce an imperial economic order that was not to the advantage of the colonies? Have we forgotten that the colonists were farmers and shopkeepers, not professional soldiers, and they faced the overwhelming might of the eighteenth-century British military, plus mercenary allies? Have we forgotten that we lost nearly every pitched battle but won an underdog's guerilla war? Have we forgotten that the British came back with greater force in the War of 1812, swept through the country, burned Washington, and savaged the people, and yet lost to our ragtag guerilla forces? Two weeks after the peace was signed, but before the news of that reached him, Andrew Jackson won the battle of New Orleans against a vastly superior marine invasion force. The Americans' hastily assembled defense included the outlaw pirates of Jean Lafitte.

This is the American mythos of the common people, often slightly outside the law that would grind them down, defending their freedom against overwhelming forces of shock and awe, defying an oppressor who seeks to constrain Americans into a larger imperial political and economic system that is not to their own perceived interest. When shall we remember this covenant of freedom and justice for the humble people that was the source of our righteousness as a nation before God, the mythos that was our moral compass?

In recent years, we invaded Iraq for no apparent legitimate reason except to force America's economic and political vision on that country, the "American Empire" as some neo-conservatives call it. Perhaps there is a better justification for our undeclared war than I can discern: the situation is complicated. Nevertheless, we went into Iraq with overwhelming military force and smashed their standing army. But the Iraqi opposition, those defending their homelands and the larger Muslim world they perceived to be under attack, mounted ever more effective guerilla actions to discredit the American occupation forces. We unwittingly turned Saddam Hussein, a thug as bad as Osama bin Laden, albeit our one-time ally, into a Robin Hood hero defending the little people against the high-tech rich and distant oppressors. Even more tragically, we let our own children in the military, for whom we pray daily, be seen around the world as like the hated imperial Sardaukar of Frank Herbert's Dune novels, who for all their technological superiority and savage training could not defeat the underground Fremen. In some parts of Iraq, we have since rebuilt resources that we had destroyed, as well as some that had been allowed to deteriorate under Saddam. Yet the more cynical among us note that, having destroyed the infrastructure of Iraq, American companies in league with the administration are allowed to get rich attempting to rebuild that infrastructure.

Our American founding mythos, itself so like the Magnificat, has been turned upside down. When will we remember that America sides with the underdog against the bully, with the right of economic self-determination rather than coercion to fit an economy that favors richer parts of the world, with the right to practice the religion of conscience? This is our true covenant as Americans. Some American prophet needs to remind us of the heritage that defines us, not the greed that defiles us.

Of course there is an American counter-mythos. The heroic general at New Orleans, Andrew Jackson, became the president who governed under the principle that to the victor belong the spoils. As many, if not more, early immigrants to America sought their personal fortune more than freedom and brotherhood. The great American entrepreneur P.T. Barnum is often credited with saying there is a sucker born every minute. Many people in the Third World say that this gospel of greed is the true American mythos, that our appeals to higher morals are hypocritical, and that American foreign behavior and domestic materialism are all the evidence needed to justify these claims. In this Advent time, when we present ourselves for judgment and look forward to the Prince of Peace, we find ourselves turned wrongly upside down, standing for the things we've always stood against. Can we be turned again?

Praise God that the Babe who is coming can make all things new. If we have turned ourselves upside down, we can be turned back right again. As Americans we can turn to side with the small people, the hungry, and the poor. God empowers us to do this by coming to us with love. We do not have to repent first so that God then will love us. God loves us before repentance and has come to proclaim that love in the Christ whose Incarnation we are about to celebrate. Of course we condemn ourselves, as my words just now were self-condemning. Not only do we condemn ourselves individually, we condemn ourselves as a people, feeling the betrayal of the religious foundation of America at some unconscious level and trumpeting a self-righteous me-first patriotism to cover up the feeling. Unrepentant self-condemnation is the ordinary condition of terror with which we live just below the level of consciousness.

God's love breaks through that. God's love does not give up. Every year the calendar comes around with Christmas, the Feast of the Incarnation. We don't have to go to God, because if we did, as unrepentant self-condemners we would not. God comes to us. God fills our lives with love's grace that overcomes the worst we can do.

The great Christian theme that God turns human expectations upside down puts the bully, the proud, the powerful, and the rich under judgment. This holds for nations as well as individuals. The infant power of the coming Babe exalts the poor, the humble, the common, the hungry, the lowly. The first will be last and the last first.

As servants of the Infant, we Christians have special obligations for our gift-giving gratitude, the other great Christian theme. Of course we gift our families and friends. Of course we gift the poor and needy in our neighborhood and city. Now we can gift those whom our upside down American policy has bullied. What a gift it would be to the Iraqi people if all American dollars for rebuilding their country were contracted to worker-owned Iraqi companies, not foreign ones! What a gift if such companies could be set up with American advisors paid by the American government rather than the companies' profits! What a gift, and statement of the Infant's Power, if the economic interests of the United States and its allies were forbidden to profit from wars like the one in Iraq, and instead the United States could implement reconciliation commissions to bring together the conflicting factions within such devastated countries and between them and their neighbors! Gratitude for God's love manifest in creation, for the evolution of human societies, and for our personal and national life should explode in gifts that manifest God's turning upside down the expectations of the proud, powerful, and rich. In the divine story of human redemption, the coming of Jesus Christ opens the way for us to be on the right side.

So now let us long for renewed fellowship with the One who gives us power to repent and turn around. Let us call for Christ to come, who judges us with truth and blesses us with mercy. Let us go toward Christmas as the celebration of giving, the heart of Christian love. Let us approach the Feast of the Incarnation with a gratitude that can turn our own lives upside down. Come to the table of the Feast to receive the gift of God. Come to the table to meet the Babe, grown, gone, and come again. Come to the table with the procession of Christians from all over the world to receive the Babe. Go from the table to deliver your gifts, which are of God. Amen.

5.

EASTER VIGIL

Luke 24:1-12
Romans 6:3-11*

THE EASTER VIGIL is a spooky time, the time after Jesus' gory death before anything happens. Of course we know what's coming. But the Vigil is just a wait for that. Luke's Gospel records that on Good Friday before sundown the women gathered some spices and prepared them to anoint Jesus. With sundown, however, the Sabbath began, and they had to wait at home, grieving and not able to do anything. After sundown on Saturday it was too dark for them to go to the tomb, and they had to wait until dawn Sunday morning—when they discovered the tomb empty. Because our Easter Vigil begins after sundown on Saturday, it technically is already Easter Day according to the Jewish reckoning of the beginning of a day. But nothing has happened yet on Saturday evening and with the end of the Sabbath not even a religious observance gives meaning to the time. How devastated the disciples must have felt in this hour! I can imagine the early Christians deep in the catacombs of Rome waiting out the Vigil by telling one another how their God is really victorious and will take care of them, appearances to the contrary notwithstanding. This place that we meet, the undercroft of the Chapel, reminds me of that as we rehearse the scriptures of salvation history, sing familiar songs, and listen to the "Romans" overhead.

One of the old traditions of the church, though not biblical, is that on Saturday between Good Friday and Easter, Jesus descended into hell, as we say in the creed, broke down its gates, kicked the bejeebers out of Satan, and freed the souls of the dead, sending them heavenward. That's called "the harrowing of hell." You can imagine, then, Jesus' return from

---

* Lections for Easter Vigil (A, B, C).

hell to Easter morning, victorious over sin, death, and the devil, a cosmic burst of energy, stopping briefly on the earth for a few resurrection appearances before launching on to heaven. The author of Ephesians has an image of Christ ascending above the highest heavens and descending into the lower parts of the earth, moving back and forth to reweave a broken cosmos. Regardless of this intriguing tradition, the disciples on the first Easter Saturday evening had no notion of victory, only of despair. They were traumatized and virtually immobile.

How has this Holy Saturday been recognized within the Christian tradition? It has been treated as the preparation for Easter morning by making it the preferred time for baptism and for joining the church. At this service people will join after a period of catechesis or learning about the church that has extended through Lent, then they will come to services the next day full of their new Christian identity, as Jesus has his full identity as risen Lord. Even the many Christians who do not attend a Vigil service think of this time as a preparation for Easter, if they mark it as holy at all.

Since ancient times, the church has used the Apostles' Creed as a baptismal formula. Catechumens were supposed to come to understand and affirm that creed, and the whole congregation that receives them in baptism recites the creed along with the new Christians or their sponsors. Insofar as the conclusion of Lent and Easter Vigil baptism is a spooky time after the crucifixion and before the resurrection, recitation of the Apostles' Creed is a little like whistling in the dark to keep up our spirits. Who are we now? We are those who

> believe in God, the Father Almighty, Creator of heaven and earth. We believe in Jesus Christ, his only Son, our Lord, who was conceived by the Holy Spirit, born of the Virgin Mary, suffered under Pontius Pilate, was crucified, died, and was buried; he descended into hell. On the third day he rose again; he ascended into heaven, is seated at the right hand of the Father, and will come again to judge the living and the dead. We believe in the Holy Spirit, the holy catholic church, the communion of saints, the forgiveness of sins, the resurrection of the body, and the life everlasting.

We are the people who organize our lives around those beliefs.

Yet we also live at great distance from the culture that produced that creed. For us, God creates the cosmos, not a cozy arrangement of the heavens above and the earth beneath. How can Jesus be the Son of the

Father if he was conceived by the Holy Spirit and born of the Virgin Mary? Many people doubt that biological account of Jesus' conception and anyway would like to see Jesus as a descendent of David, which would require Joseph to be his father. We are not likely to believe that if we dug a deep enough mine into the earth, we would arrive at hell, and we do not believe that heaven in the religious sense is up. Do we really imagine heavenly Jesus and God the Father sitting side by side? I could go on and on in this vein, enumerating the many qualifications and symbolic reinterpretations that we today would put upon the Apostles' Creed, so many that many contemporary Christians metaphorically cross their fingers when saying the creed. The creed is not a literal statement of our theology. If it were, we could not believe it and live fully engaged with the world as we know it. A literal affirmation of the Apostles' Creed would put us in bad faith.

How far can we move from the literal to the metaphorical and still keep to the heart of the church's affirmations? That is a good question, but it is essentially out of place. The function of the creed is not, as so many people have thought, to be a brief summary of Christian theology. Perhaps it once was that, but we need real theology to perform that function now. The creed will not perform that function. Rather, the function of the recitation of the Apostles' Creed is to affirm our solidarity with those entering into the Christian life, with the line of Christians from the earliest days to our own, with the panoply of different kinds of Christians in all places who still recite the creed. Reciting the creed in a liturgy is what philosophers call a "performative linguistic act." When the bride and groom in a wedding say, "I do," they are not describing their willingness to marry: those words make the marriage. When we recite the creed, we are not describing our beliefs, except in a very vague sense: we are performing our unity with Christians of all times and places. The Apostles' Creed works for that function precisely because we think it once was what Christians believed about God the Father, Son, and Holy Spirit, or thought they did. For the Apostles' Creed to work as a gesture of unity, we deliberately have to forget that creeds in the ancient world were used to exclude Christians who disagreed with the majority. The Apostles' Creed is a good choice because it seems never to have been used in a major council to exclude large groups of Christians the way the Nicene and Chalcedonian creeds were.

Now you must have noticed that these musings on the ambiguities of the Apostles' Creed are not the upbeat fare that you were hoping for in the

Easter Vigil when we celebrate all God has done for us and all God will do in the future. The reason for these ambiguous musings is that preparation for Easter is only half the story of this Holy Saturday, this spooky day. The other half is the traumatized grief at the collapse and corruption of the great hopes of Jesus. The sweep toward Easter makes us forget the downside of the moment.

So reflect with me about the creed from the downside for a moment.

God the Father Almighty, Creator of heaven and earth, has given us a world where stars burn out, where the innocent suffer greatly, where human pain is almost unbearable, and where we all will die. We ourselves are materially fortunate. But we all know people whose heavenly Father has given them stones rather than bread. We have to admit that Saturday truth.

Belief in Jesus Christ, who was ennobled by divine parentage and victorious over hell, has motivated the most warlike of all the major religions, save perhaps Islam (which got it from us). Christianity became Rome's religion because emperor Constantine thought it won him a battle. The crusades were gratuitous evil launched upon the people of Palestine, trampling Byzantine civilization in the process. Belief in the Lordship of Christ brought the nations of Europe to such bloody conflict that they achieved peace only by attempting to make religious belief a private thing. The promotion of belief in Jesus Christ legitimated European colonialism. Warmongers among Christians today out-shout the shrill cries of the terrorists. All this, however more complex than what I've just said, is a Saturday truth.

What shall we say about the beneficence of belief in the Holy Spirit? The holy catholic church is not unified, or catholic, but divided into countless sects. The saints are not in fact in communion with one another, but often at war. Some sins might be forgiven, but I can't think of many if you look at the attitudes of many Christians toward the poor, the different, and the hostile. The resurrection of the body, for so many, has come to mean the perfection of the body, and belief in life everlasting has become an excuse for making people tolerate intolerable conditions in this life. These, too, are Saturday truths.

The view from Saturday of Good Friday's griefs shows the downside. Jesus the charismatic teacher is dead. The God he worshiped created a hellhole for many people. The religion about Jesus is an institution of extraordinary harm as well as good. The Spirit he sent to guide us deals with institutions of corruption. We need to sit with these Saturday truths. They are the truths of the cross. If we rush too quickly to Easter, we will find ourselves lying about God, beating people up with our triumphalist religion, and congratulating ourselves on a spiritual status for our ways of Christian life that they do not deserve. Without acknowledging the trauma of the cross, we will have a fake Easter.

I invite you to a truer Easter faith that affirms God as Creator of the whole cosmos, the bad as well as the good, and who still can be loved as Jesus loved the Father who abandoned him on the cross. I invite you to a truer Easter faith that affirms a risen Christ who sets the cross always before us, who does not lead us to war but to humility, who is the judge of us all and especially of what is done in his Name. I invite you to a truer Easter faith that finds Christ's risen body within the shards of the divided church, that smashes our pretensions to authenticity that keep us from uniting with saints on the other side, that insists that forgiveness of sins be the hard work of transformation, that refuses resurrection hope without crucifixion, and that offers life everlasting only within the eternal life of God. I invite you to keep vigil with me to ponder the gravity Saturday's truths give Sunday's songs. Amen.

CONVERSION

6.

A NEW AWAKENING

Isaiah 62:1-5
1 Corinthians 12:1-11
*John 2:1-11**

TODAY'S COLLEGE STUDENTS probably like John's story of the wedding at Cana better than did the very sober Christians of my youth. What do we learn from the story? First and most obviously, Jesus liked to party. The names of the married couple are not mentioned, and we can assume from the story that they are friends of Jesus' mother rather than Jesus himself. Cana is nine miles from Jesus' home, and that is a long walk if you don't like parties for strangers. We know from the story that Mary, too, liked to party because she was the one who had been told by the steward that the wine had run out. We learn from the story that Jesus didn't want to use any special powers but did so because his mother insisted, sort of a caricature of the relationship between a Jewish mother and her son. Not only were Mary and Jesus not teetotalers but also we don't see much of the discipline of moderation. If we suppose that the host had ordered and served the wine he expected to be sufficient for the party, then Mary and Jesus must have been having a good time, which they wanted to continue, for them to want to make more. Now if you calculate six water jars holding 20 to 30 gallons apiece, filled to the brim, that's between 120 and 180 gallons of top quality wine from Jesus the Good Vintner. It's a good thing they had a nine-mile walk back home. Psalm 104 says that, among the great things of creation, God made wine to gladden the human heart, and this must have been a glad party to end all parties, even if the married couple seems peripheral to the story.

---

* Lections for the Second Sunday after Epiphany, Year C.

Nevertheless, the sober Christians of my youth were somewhat uncomfortable with this story, and with good reason. Whereas wine might have been the preferred beverage in rural Galilee because they didn't have much clean drinking water, we know the damage drinking can do when drivers drink, when excessive drinking ruins health, when inappropriate drinking ruins work, projects, friendships, and families; we know alcoholism to be a serious disease, something not at all understood in Jesus' time. It might be strange to hear me say in this instance that you should not do what Jesus did but rather what your parents, the administration at your college, and others have told you: don't drink if you are underage and drink in careful moderation if you are old enough; know also that a little alcohol might lead you to do things you wouldn't do when sober and for which you nevertheless are responsible. So why then is this over-the-top party story in the Bible, especially at such a pivotal place in John's Gospel?

The clue is in the first four words of the first sentence: "On the third day there was a wedding in Cana of Galilee." The third day from what? It was the third day from the calling of the core disciples, whom Jesus then brought to the wedding. John's Gospel has a different account of the calling of the disciples from Matthew, Mark, and Luke who describe a seaside calling of fishermen. In John's account, Jesus went to be baptized by John the Baptist at Bethany, near Jerusalem. There he met two disciples of John the Baptist whom the Baptist sent to get acquainted with Jesus. One of those was likely John, the brother of James, by repute the eventual author of John's Gospel and traditionally identified with the Beloved Disciple. The other was Andrew, Peter's brother. The two disciples of John the Baptist were so impressed with Jesus that Andrew found his brother Peter, who apparently also had been involved with the baptizing phenomenon, and brought him to Jesus. The next day Jesus left the Jerusalem area for Galilee and found Philip, who was a neighbor of Andrew and Peter. Philip then found Nathanael who confessed Jesus to be the Son of God and the King of Israel.

Jesus took his new band of disciples to the wedding at Cana. The Gospel does not record that Jesus took them first to a mountaintop for an exhilarating new experience, as happened later at the Transfiguration. He did not take them off to pray. He did not preach or lecture to them or take them to a communal meal. The first thing he did with the disciples, according to John, was to take them to a wedding party and make sure they enjoyed it.

John's Gospel differs from the others in being the last written and having the heaviest theological interpretation. Although John is likely to be the most accurate historically, it is written from the standpoint of people who already know the end of the story. The end of the story, as John tells it, is that Jesus has triumphed over the world, that he made a place for his disciples with God, that he himself is with God and has sent the Holy Spirit to be with his followers forever. The point of John's Gospel is that God has triumphed in Christ and that God's Holy Spirit is with the people to see them through. So God's victory should be celebrated right off with a party. Although the disciples could not understand it at the time, Jesus initiated their ministry with a celebration of God's victory. That the party celebrates a wedding, with an unnamed bridal party, prefigures or symbolizes the marriage between God and God's people. The real bridal party is God and Israel, God and the disciples, God and the church, indeed God and the whole world including the Gentiles.

The story of the wedding in Cana is the first of a series of increasingly complex and startling miracles that Jesus performs in John's narrative, ending with the raising of Lazarus from the dead and finally Jesus' own resurrection. All along the way people who do not understand Jesus slowly come to do so. Remember poor Nicodemus who thought he had to return to the womb to be born again in the Spirit? The closing scene of John's Gospel is the fish breakfast Jesus cooked for his disciples after they thought he was dead. He healed the spirit of poor Peter, who had denied him three times, by getting him to say three times that he loved Jesus. He told Peter to feed those whom Jesus loved. Peter asked Jesus about Jesus' special relationship with the Beloved Disciple, and Jesus responded to the effect that it was none of Peter's business because Jesus' relationship with each person is different, a poignant lesson with which to end the Gospel.

Now I am not asking you to believe in miracles, turning water to wine, multiplying loaves and fishes, healing the sick, or raising the dead. What to believe about miracles is a very important topic for another time. But I am asking you to live in God's time after the first party. Or rather, regard this time as our party of the Christian life, even if our time looks like anything but a party. This is our time, like the disciples in their time, for learning what it means to be God's people, and we shall make foolish mistakes before we get it down. Living in God's world is not what we might expect. Great armies do not come down to drive out the Romans or protect us from terrorists. Too many Christians defend racism rather than remove it. The Christian movement is not a government that rules with righteousness; in fact, it has to live subversively with governments that usually are not righteous, just as the early Christians did. The strong and proud are not our real leaders, the humble and poor are: witness Martin Luther King Jr. In so many ways, the Christian life is lived contrary to all expectations of victory and greatness. Resurrection to spiritual life is obtained through spiritual crucifixion, through suffering the blind and evil powers of the world, and through keeping the faith when all hope is given up.

How do we awaken to this strange, upside down story of Christianity? We've heard it so often it no longer startles us. Many answers to that question exist. Sometimes world events shock us so that we ask with new urgency what it means to be a Christian. I remember the shock of Dr. King's assassination, and with several other ministers in my area preached on the Grapes of Wrath the next Sunday. The events of 9/11 and the war in Iraq had that effect for many. Sometimes a vision of the poor lets us see Jesus. Sometimes we meet a person or group who startles us to awareness of the seriousness of Christianity. For many of us, it takes a tragedy such as the death or serious illness of someone close. What I want to urge today, however, is none of these stimuli from the outside. I ask instead that we turn inward and inquire how it is with our souls. Isn't that the question you should ask of your best friends, in order to be a friend yourself? Of course such questions are embarrassing, and only the best of friends can ask that question straightforwardly. But asking the question of ourselves does not involve embarrassment, only confusion, shock, sometimes grief, and sometimes joy.

"How is it with my soul?" is a very Methodist question. I have urged us not to settle for being what John Wesley called an "almost Christian." Wesley preached a sermon in 1741 called "The Almost Christian" in which he distinguished that from the "altogether Christian." An almost Christian has what Wesley called the "heathen virtues" of morality and a strong regard for justice, truth, and giving assistance or charity to one another. An almost Christian also has the "form of Christian godliness," by which Wesley meant living by the stringent moral code of the New Testament and participating in all the means of grace in the church, including private prayer. From the outside, an almost Christian can look very like an altogether Christian. But what is lacking, he said, is inner sincerity. When we look into our soul, you and I, do we recognize deep sincerity?

Sincerity, Wesley said, involves three things. First it involves genuine love of God, not sentimental feelings of gratitude but genuine love. Loving God is very difficult because God's creation involves destruction as well as construction. Second, sincerity involves loving our neighbors, not just behaving charitably toward them, not just being good to them. Sincerity involves genuinely loving them, which is a disposition of the heart that can be difficult when our neighbors are our enemies. Third, sincerity involves real faith in the inward heart. By faith, Wesley did not mean just belief, although true understanding is part of faith. Wesley had a quaint way of making this point. He said that devils, because of their supernatural knowledge, know the truth of all the Christian history, witness, and doctrines, including that Christ had died for their salvation. Yet they are still devils because their hearts do not accept that salvation. What the devils lack, perfect theologians that they are, is the inward acceptance of God's saving love and the rejoicing, the returning of God's love, and the loving of neighbor out of the excess of joy.

This brings us to the wedding at Cana. An altogether Christian, sincere in loving God, loving neighbor, and rejoicing in the convictions of faith, knows that discipleship is a party. We usually don't understand how it is a party—coming to understand how it is, is part of discipleship. It usually does not look or feel like a party—most of Jesus' disciples were martyred and he himself was crucified. Our own lives are filled with many confusions, failures, and betrayals of others, of ourselves, of our ideals, of our Christ, just like Peter's. Yet in loving God in total sincerity, and loving neighbors in total sincerity, and abiding in the deepest faith in which God dwells wildly and joyfully, the altogether Christian knows that this life is a party given by God. It is our very own wedding party.

Wesley knew his sermon had a little trick to it. Most of us are not anywhere near being even an almost Christian. We aren't very moral, truthful, just, or even fully observant of the forms of the Christian life. The point is that if we get the sincerity, that which distinguishes an altogether Christian from the almost Christian, then the virtues of the almost Christian will come along in time. Begin with the sincere love of God, the sincere love of neighbor, and the sincere faith that God's love and power for salvation already reside in your heart, and all the rest will be added through the practices of sanctification. Love and faith come first, and they are available now.

So I ask you about your soul. Do you find there sincere love of God and neighbor, the joyful faith in God's love and power? That question might take a long time to answer. I invite you into the Christian life in which that faithful sincerity can be awakened and made to glow.

Back to the wedding at Cana. Given that Jesus was instructing his disciples to become aware of the love of God and the fulfillment of being a disciple within God's world, I'm sure that the Good Vintner used the 30-gallon containers and made a full 180 gallons of the very best wine. Amen.

7.

WISE MEN (AN EPIPHANY SERMON)

Isaiah 60:1-6
Ephesians 3:1-12
*Matthew 2:1-12**

WELCOME TO THE new year. I hope that you all enjoyed the holiday season and that the diets you swore to a few days ago are still in effect. We all know, of course, that the holiday season is very difficult for many people, and we look for ways to ease their pain. We hope this year will bring a global peace that eluded us in years past, as well as a sense of direction in a world that seems to be based on greed, from the nation's geopolitical extremes to our personal habits.

For Christians, today is not only the first Sunday of the new year but also, more importantly, Epiphany Sunday. Epiphany celebrates the appearance of Jesus Christ to the world, and the traditional text is the story of the three wise men who were the first strangers to pay him homage.

Wise men were not in good supply in the first century, and even with the recent addition of wise women, we still suffer from a short supply in the twenty-first. Late-modern society requires a good education, especially in technical fields, yet too many of our people lack the education even to be steady unskilled laborers. Democracy requires both a broad background and a refined capacity to learn new things and evaluate competing opinions, yet too many of us are merely parochial and cannot understand issues more complex than our immediate environment. Happiness in personal life requires knowing how to take satisfaction in our lives, in the lives of others, in the arts, the sciences, and public affairs,

---

* Lections for Epiphany Sunday, Year C.

yet consumerist culture persuades us that satisfaction is impossible without more commodities. Our nation wields enormous economic and military power to impose the government's will on others, yet without understanding from the perspective of those others what would be genuinely good or bad for them. Our cultural wisdom seems to be asleep!

My particular concern as a Christian pastor is with the short supply of wisdom in our religious life. One of the glories of our age is the magnificent advance in scientific understanding of nature, yet too many popular theologies ask us to believe what we know to be false. Another of our glories is a fantastic explosion in the plastic and visual arts, literature, poetry, drama, dance, and music, fed by a wonderful confluence of world cultures and freed from the pieties of both Enlightenment rationalism and dogmatic religion, yet popular theologies insist on a simplistic picture of human nature we know to be false. The rock-bottom conviction of the Christian faith is that the world is God's creature, yet popular theologies ask us to believe in a God so small that the breadth and depth of creation cannot possibly be God's creature. The human predicament addressed by the Christian faith is that our hearts are sinful, yet too many theologies simply aim to make us feel good. Jesus Christ asks us to love God with all our heart, mind, soul, and strength, yet too many theologies say it is belief that counts or conspicuous membership in so-called Christian culture. Jesus Christ asks us to love our neighbors, to love those different from ourselves, to love the poor and culturally excluded, indeed to love our enemies, yet too many theologies say we should love first the church. They say we should think for the church, act within the church, be first of all for the church, because the church is what Stanley Hauerwas calls a band of "resident aliens," God's people enduring a foreign land. To the contrary, the church is a bearer of God to the world, the church is for the sake of the world, the church should invite all the peoples of the world into the hospitality of God, as Henk Pieterse says, not into the limited hospitality of the church.

The result of too much sleepy theology is that the Christian movement is split by culture wars between conservative and liberals. It falls prey to patriotic enthusiasm when those aliens and enemies should be its loving concern. It neglects the poor and needy. It fails to see what God's hospitality would be for those of other cultures. It fails to engage the infinite passions of our heart with God rather than self-interest. It leads us to believe that the limits of the relevant world are what we can own and control. It blinds us to the shattering criticisms that the arts make of our

defensive self-images. It alienates us from the understanding of God's creation, which is the beginning of true piety. It presents us pictures of a
domesticated God when God in fact is wild beyond measure. Too many
sleepy theologies have made the church unwise. The official way to say
this is that the church has lost the Mind of Christ.

Of course I exaggerate. The Christian church has many wise thinkers
and leaders. So do other religions. Nevertheless wisdom does not now
inform the church in the complex ways needed because we seem to have
a childish terror of the complexities of life. Too many believe we need a
simple theology, because people are simple. So instead of thinking
through the complexities and ambiguities of cultural life, we sell the simple falsehood that you just need to sign up with the conservatives or liberals. Instead of the painful process of coming to see through the eyes of
others, we half-guiltily advocate our own tradition as the only way. Instead
of tracing carefully how our social system makes some people poor, we
promote feel-good charity. Instead of patiently inquiring what form of religion would be salvific for people different from ourselves, we let ourselves
believe a one-size-fits-all piety will do. Instead of stretching our minds to
know God through the vast reaches of space and time and to love God
with a love that overcomes disappointment and death, we think of God as
a nice, just king who will make things come out all right according to our
conception of rewards. We settle for puny, simplistic symbols even though
the divine Logos with which we are given to think dares to think the
unthinkable.

The Epiphany story in the Gospel of John reads something like this: "In
the beginning was the Logos, and the Logos was with God, and the Logos
was God . . . What has come into being in him was life, and the life was the
light of all people. The light shines in the darkness, and the darkness did
not overcome it . . . The true light, which enlightens everyone, was coming
into the world . . . He came to what was his own, and his own people did
not accept him. But to all who received him, who believed in his name, he
gave power to become children of God, who were born, not of blood or of
the will of the flesh or of the will of man, but of God." We need a new
awakening of wisdom for Christianity to be true to its light, its Logos.
Otherwise we cannot be born of God, only of some simplistic fake god.

Now you surely have a sense of humor about this, knowing that I am a
professor of philosophy, religion, and theology and am preaching from a
university pulpit. What else can a person such as I say? Most ordinary
parishes would not tolerate such a plea for more responsible Christian

intellect. They would say my stance is elitist. But remember that Jesus' first devotees were the wise men from the East. The Epiphany of Christ was first to the wise. The wise were the first to enlist. Remember also that the First Great Awakening, in the eighteenth century, was started by people like John and Charles Wesley at Oxford, gathering fellow students for prayer and a mission to the poor; the leader of the American side of the First Great Awakening was Jonathan Edwards, America's greatest theologian, whose last job was to be president of the college we now call Princeton. The Second Great Awakening, in the nineteenth century, took its start at Yale under the leadership of Yale's president, Timothy Dwight, who was Edward's grandson. If a Third Great Awakening should come from a university, that would not be surprising to those who know the importance of wisdom for loving God.

Christian wisdom to awaken our time must embrace all that can be known in the university and elsewhere, else we fail the Logos from which we have our being. Of course our knowledge is fallible, often little better than well-entrenched hypotheses; this holds for theology as well. For this very reason Christian wisdom should seek out any domain of inquiry that might correct it. That theology is best that makes itself vulnerable to correction from every angle, adjusts itself to well-taken criticism, and steadies itself through learning from all sources of knowledge. I myself am convinced that most theologies that have had any currency whatsoever have had an important truth for someone in some context; theologies conflict with one another and become genuinely false when they are generalized beyond those contexts. Sometimes in desperate prayer, an image of a domesticated God is just fine but a domesticated God cannot be creator of this wild cosmos. The theological job of Christian wisdom is not so much to pick one theology to defend against all others, as happened in the First and Second Great Awakenings, as it is to understand the different contexts in which different symbolic expressions are true and the contexts in which they are false. Genuine theology embraces and articulates all the ways in which God can be engaged truly and guides the people in all of their contexts.

I have not been talking about the difference between a wise intelligence and a foolish or stupid intelligence. Rather I have been complaining about a sleeping intelligence and calling for an awakening of that intelligence. The Christian tradition, like most others, is filled with wisdom that once was awake and vital. My complaint has been that many of those who should have been awake and vital with Christian wisdom—others can speak for other traditions—have been asleep. Christian wisdom has become too disconnected from the sciences and arts, too inward looking when it should make itself vulnerable to the world, too defensive of past identity. Sleeping wisdom leads to foolish behavior. I ask for a revitalization of Christianity in the twenty-first century starting with an awakening of wisdom to its role, a role that engages the best we know, that embraces all those whom we should love, and that rejects simple ideas that merely reflect our own image back to us in favor of the complex inquiry that lets us find the image of God in the infinitely dense creation. To be born of God is to love the light and Logos of God. The first Epiphany of our Lord is as divine wisdom.

I invite you, therefore, to participate in a Great Awakening of wisdom. A new Great Awakening must also awaken fervor, and witness, and new direction, and new discipline. But the Third Great Awakening begins with awakening wisdom, and perhaps in a university. If your mind hungers for honest truth and is offended by the simplemindedness of the theologies you have heard, come to an awakening of Christian wisdom that will unfold a more realistic, complex way. If your moral strength hungers to bring justice to a world more complex than slogans, come to an awakening of Christian wisdom that sorts that out. If your soul hungers for meaning in an age when even religion seems to be a commodity, come to an awakening of Christian wisdom that participates in the deepest mysteries. If your heart hungers to know God, and to be known by God, come to an awakening of Christian wisdom that dares to touch the unthinkable, that dares to be penetrated by the Logos of God, that dares to be vulnerable to God's wild love, that dares the ecstasy of divine knowledge in our flesh. For we cannot pray unless we have the thoughts with which to witness the divine immensity. The wise men witnessed the Epiphany. Amen.

8.

SAMARITANS AND OTHER ALIENS

Amos 7:7-17
*Luke 10:25-37**

I N ONE OF the most arresting images in biblical literature, Amos says that God stands in the midst of the people with a plumb line. Builders use a string with a weight on the bottom, a plumb line, to determine whether a wall is vertical and straight. Less subjective than eyeballing the wall and governed by the cosmic force of gravity, a plumb line is an absolute measure. God stands in the midst of the people with an absolute measure for their deeds, and Amos quotes God saying that, because of this measure, he would destroy both the religious and political establishment of Israel. Amos does not say God is just thinking about destroying Israel— he really is going to do this. God is not into tough love, for Amos. Justice is the order of the day.

We do not like this harsh "Old Testament" God, believing as most of us do that God is loving, rather the way we dream our mothers were loving. Often we think, or hope, that divine judgment is nothing but God's efforts to get us to do better. Yet there is something very important in the plumb line image. Who and what we are before God is our absolute identity. No excuses. No extenuating circumstances. No promises of doing better tomorrow. Moreover, divine judgment is not something to come later, postponed by a long life. As Amos says, God is even now holding the plumb line in the midst of the people. We live before God absolutely every day of our lives, whether we know it or not. One of the earliest heresies in Christianity, called Marcionism after its founder Marcion, said that the

---

* Lections for Proper 10, Sunday between July 10 and July 16, Year C.

harsh God of the Old Testament was evil and that Christian should believe only in the Super Loving High God. Marcionism was quickly condemned, however difficult it was for Christians to reconcile the God of judgment with the God of Love.

A profound reason exists to pay attention to the God with the plumb line. Unless we are held responsible in an absolute sense for who and what we are, we have no self. If we relativize ourselves with excuses from the past, or promises for the future, we ourselves turn out to be personally absent. Our moral self reduces to the conditions within which we live, the influences of others upon us, and the limitations of our bodies. Although, of course, we live within such conditions, influences, and limitations, our moral selves consist in what we make of them. Our moral selves develop through time, maturing from childhood, with many starts and stops, with repentance and promise of doing better. Yet at any time, who we are, indeed who we are over our lifetime, is what we make of ourselves within the conditions, influences, and limitations given us. This is our true self, our true identity, our soul, and we comprehend this only when we imagine standing in absolute perspective before God, who is in our midst with the plumb line.

The Christian gospel is that divine judgment is not the whole of the story, and it is not the whole story for Amos and Judaism: the God of justice is also the God of mercy. Among the most important elements in the development of a moral self are the occasions in which we respond with repentance before God and with gratitude for mercy. Sometimes we imagine God to be in time because our true selves develop in interaction with the ultimate divine perspective. Yet imagining God to be temporal, to be a being within time, always runs the risk of domesticating the eternal majesty of the God who creates time itself. The true absolutely ultimate God before whom we become our true selves is the eternal God within whose plenitude we live as temporal beings with eternal life.

Jesus was asked, according to Luke, what one must do to inherit eternal life. He did not answer with a metaphysical discourse on the eternal God, which you were afraid just now that I was about to inflict upon you. Rather, Jesus turned the question: What does it say in the Bible? The questioner, a lawyer, answered by citing the line from Deuteronomy 4 that you should love the Lord your God with all your heart, mind, soul, and strength, combining this with the line from Leviticus 19 that you should love your neighbor as your self. "Right," said Jesus. When Matthew and Mark tell this story, they put the lines from scripture in Jesus' mouth, not that of the lawyer. It must have been Jesus' central teaching about the law and justice.

According to Luke, the lawyer did not let the matter lie, but questioned Jesus about who his neighbor was. Commentators suggest that he meant to limit his liability by circumscribing those who counted as neighbors. Jesus responded with the famous parable of the good Samaritan. You know the story. A man was badly mugged while traveling to Jericho and was left by the side of the road. Two religious people came by, a priest and a Levite, who had religious responsibilities to all the people of Israel. They did not want to get involved and passed by on the other side of the road. A Samaritan came by who pitied the man, took him to a hotel, tended his wounds, and said he would pay for the man's recovery. The lawyer, when questioned, said it was the Samaritan who had been the neighbor, and Jesus said to him, "Go and do likewise."

Jesus' point, of course, was that the people with the ethnic and religious obligation to the victim were not real neighbors. The real neighbor was the Samaritan who was ethnically as well as religiously alien. In fact, relations between Jews and Samaritans were worse than alienated, they were hostile. Although he was himself an observant Jew, Jesus had little patience with ethnic or religious differences. As Luke pointed out, Jesus took his mission to Samaritan as well as Jewish towns. According to the Gospel of John, Jesus talked with a Samaritan woman, which was forbidden, offered her the water of life, and told her that religious differences make no difference when God is worshiped in spirit and in truth. Jesus healed Canaanites and Romans also. Although he was slow to come to this conclusion, ethnic and religious identities did not count.

What counted for Jesus is loving people. Paul in Romans 13 and again in Galatians 5 says that loving neighbor as self sums up all the law. The Epistle of James says the same thing. The Gospel of John does not cite the line about loving neighbors from Leviticus, but it argues even more forcefully that Jesus' work and identity were to teach people to love one another despite qualities that would justify indifference or hate. Love is the very center of the Christian gospel, and it was recognized as such from Jesus' time down to today.

With respect to divine judgment, then, the inference seems clear. What is the plumb line by which we are judged? For Amos, it was the law, and for Jesus and the Christians it was love as the summary of the law. In fact, where law means social and religious patterns that distinguish one group from another, as was clearly the case in much of the Torah, love trumps those differences. Jesus relativized the law, in the sense of religious patterns, to faithfulness to love.

Who are we before God? We essentially are lovers, good lovers or bad lovers. People who do not make lovers of themselves in the midst of the conditions, influences, and limitations of life have no self. No soul. Actually, that cannot be quite right. Everyone is held responsible in ultimate perspective, even if people utterly fail at responsibility. So we should say that everyone has a self or soul: the worry is whether it is happily loving or wretched, blessed or damned. Our eternal life depends on how we are lovers, said Jesus.

To love our own kind is easy, especially when they love us back. The Samaritans and other aliens teach us to love in the hard cases. Like the good Samaritan, truly responsible lovers are those whose love extends to those who are alien to them, especially those whom others have failed to love. We learn the hard lessons of love when aliens, from whom we should expect indifference or hate, love us instead. Thank God for aliens! Now according to Jesus, we are to love God, as well as neighbors, with all our heart, mind, soul, and strength. Who, for us, is more alien than God? How can we love the eternal Creator whose plumb line holds us in judgment? How can we love the Creator who gives us conditions of life filled with war and poverty, influences from people who would warp the soul, limitations of disease and death, all the ambiguities of the environment from which we present ourselves to God?

Some people say we love in trade. Because God loves us, we love God. Yet God's ordinary treatment of human kind is very mixed, loving benefits, yes, but also indifference and sometimes hateful punishment. We can no more liken God's true love as Creator to a human lover, such as the good Samaritan, than we can think of God's eternity as the time of a dialogue partner. How hard it is for us to appreciate that even the hardships, suffering, and death of life, especially innocent life, are the creatures of a loving Creator. Yet there is some sublime loveliness in the Creator that transfigures all these considerations. The one who holds the plumb line and calls us to account can become our Beloved. We do not love God by willing to do so. What we will is that God help us. Yet by learning to love the unlovely among our neighbors, we can attain that integrity of self, that maturity of soul, which lets us take God as our lover.

Charles Albert Tindley, the great African-American hymn writer, understood this subtle transformation: we begin by crying to God for help and end up becoming God's lover when help fails. His extraordinary hymn,

Stand By Me, starts with nature's brute forces: "When the storms of life are raging, stand by me. When the storms of life are raging, stand by me. When the world is tossing me, like a ship upon the sea, thou who rulest wind and water, stand by me." It moves to human struggle: "In the midst of tribulation, stand by me. In the midst of tribulation, stand by me. When the host of hell assail, and my strength begins to fail, thou who never lost a battle, stand by me." Then to personal failings: "In the midst of faults and failures, stand by me. In the midst of faults and failures, stand by me. When I've done the best I can, and my friends misunderstand, thou who knowest all about me, stand by me." Then oppression and enmity: "In the midst of persecution, stand by me. In the midst of persecution, stand by me. When my foes in war array undertake to stop my way, thou who saved Paul and Silas, stand by me." Tindley knew that God does not calm all seas, protect us from all defeat, reverse our failures, or give us all victories. The most fortunate among us just get old. Verse five says: "When I'm growing old and feeble, stand by me; when I'm growing old and feeble, stand by me. When my life becomes a burden, and I'm nearing chilly Jordan, O thou Lily of the Valley, stand by me." Readers of the Song of Solomon know that the Lily of the Valley is the Beloved, not a champion, but the Beloved. Somehow Tindley moved from demanding that God behave like a good Samaritan to singing that God, his Beloved, receive his love. To love God with all our heart, mind, soul, and strength is to be able to take God as our lover. As we come closer to the Lily of the Valley, we also embrace the plumb line in our midst. Amen.

GROWTH

WHAT TO DO WITH SIN

1 Samuel 1:4-20
Hebrews 10:11-25
Mark 13:1-8
1 Samuel 2:1-10
Luke 1:46-55*

MOST OF THE time we preachers deal with topics so mysterious that we don't really know what we are talking about or with topics requiring so much specialized expertise of sorts we lack that we speak in ignorance. Yet we must address those topics in order to remain true to the gospel. Today's topic is different, however: sin. Sin is no mystery, and I am expert in it. Sin comes up at this moment in the Christian calendar because Advent is only two weeks away and sin is that from which the advent of Jesus Christ is supposed to save us. The text from 1 Samuel was used by Christians to prefigure the birth of Jesus: Hannah is a bit like Mary, and little Samuel grew up to save Israel. Mary's song, the Magnificat, in Luke 1 is a self-conscious parallel to Hannah's song of thanksgiving in 1 Samuel 2. Our text from Mark is an apocalyptic discussion of waiting for Jesus' second coming, a premature topic when we haven't considered the first coming yet. Today the Word of God is about the human condition and how Jesus stands in relation to that.

Sin is a double offense, outward and inward. Most obviously sin is an offense because of the harm it does to people or things. What to do with this aspect of sin is, first, to avoid sinning, second, to make amends when you have sinned, and, third, to expect to pay an appropriate price for the harm done others, our environment, our institutions, or ourselves.

---

* The first four passages are lections for Proper 28, Sunday between November 13 and November 19, Year B.

The second kind of offense is that in sinning we make ourselves into sinners, compromising the contributions we might make to the righteousness of the cosmos and presenting us before God as deviant from the holiness we should have in gratitude for creation. Whereas the first, outward, aspect of sin is a moral problem, the second aspect is religious, sin against the inward heart. The religious dimension of sin is that it alienates us from the Ground of our Being that gives us a context in which we both are free enough to be responsible and are surrounded by choices in which our obligation is to choose the best option insofar as we can know that.

The religious problem is what to do with the religious offense in sinning. Ancient Israel understood the situation this way. God had laid down on Mount Sinai an elaborate set of rules for what we would call both moral and cultic or ethnic behavior. The Ten Commandments and many other rules are moral in our sense of the term. Rules about what foods are unclean and should not be eaten, or what kinds of fabric you can combine in a garment, are cultic or ethnic, special practices that distinguished Israel from the surrounding nations. Because Israel was ordained to be a whole nation of priests, according to the covenant with Moses, its very identity depended on keeping the rules of the covenant. Of course, infractions of the covenantal rules were inevitable, and often unintentional. So in addition to prescriptions to pay for the sins where possible respecting the outward offense of sin, the Mosaic covenant established a variety of ritual sacrifices that restore the individual offender and the whole people to a right relation with God. The priests who conduct the sacrifices are the people's special representatives to God.

This situation is a profound expression of God's seemingly conflicting traits of righteousness and mercy. On the one hand, God sets up the covenantal rules for right living before the righteous divine majesty, thus in effect establishing the ways by which people can become alienated from the divine majesty, sin in the sense of breaking the covenantal conditions. On the other hand, God sets up the atoning sacrifices that allow sinners to be returned to right relation with God, restoring Israel to the status of a nation of pure and holy priests who can approach the divine majesty. God is righteously demanding and yet merciful to sinners.

We sophisticated late-modern people—some of you might even be postmodern—are likely not to be able to take the ancient account of Israel's covenant at face value. Many people today are unwilling to believe in a God they believe sets up rules to trip us and then condescendingly establishes ways to pick us up again. Such an image of God is not only too anthropomorphic but it also depicts God as an adolescent. Yet I ask you to think outside the scriptural language for a minute.

We find ourselves in a world filled with things and ways with varying values. Because we are free to choose among different ways to go, we know that some of those ways are destructive to important values and others are productive to them. Some options are better than others. Situations sometimes are so complex that it is hard to tell which are the better choices. Most often, however, we do know what is right and what is wrong. We are obligated to choose the better course precisely because that is the better course to choose: that's the meaning of obligation. When we do the worse rather than the better, there are two results. The first is that the world is worse off by our choice than it would be had we chosen differently. The second is that we make ourselves into bad choosers. We give ourselves the moral character of being the people who made these wrong choices when we could have made better ones. Rarely is our moral character wholly determined by one choice. It develops over a lifetime of choices, some bad, some good, some important, others trivial, some made with deliberate intent, some with thoughtless inadvertence. Moral character is extremely complex. Yet it is what we make of ourselves through the lifetime of conditions in which we have to live. Although throughout our lives we are connected to other people and environing conditions in many ways, and most of our actions are not ours alone—we act conjointly with others—the one thing for which we have sole responsibility is the building of our own moral character.

Deep in our heart each of us knows that our moral identity is who we are before God, who we are in ultimate perspective. Our moral character in this sense is our religious identity. We know we are responsible for it, and we have a good idea just what our character is. And it is terrifying. In our best moments we rush to do better and make amends for our sins, that is, to deal with the first, outward, offense of sin, the actual harm done. Even if our efforts at amendment are successful, however, the moral character we previously created for ourselves remains, only to be supplemented by new virtue, not erased.

And so we talk fast to persuade ourselves and others that our own moral character is not important. We talk about the causes served and the harms done, calling attention away from ourselves. If circumstances push hard at us we explain ourselves as pawns of the forces of history, as the products of problematic families, as victims of a deprived environment, as participants in a story where others are the powerful agents. The faster we talk, the less convincing we are. We can't stop talking because we know that if we did we would hear the truth. Yet we become anxious because we realize we are in denial. We can't sit still because of our need to be occupied with busyness that distracts us from the inner life. But as we fall asleep at night or wake in the morning, as our thought-controls loosen, the truth sneaks up on us. It's like suddenly meeting God the Judge: we are caught naked.

> Where can I go from your spirit? Or where can I flee from your
>   presence?
> If I ascend to heaven, you are there; if I make my bed in Sheol, you are
>   there.
> If I take the wings of the morning and settle at the farthest limits of the
>   sea,
> Even there your hand shall lead me, and your right hand shall hold me
>   fast.
> If I say, 'Surely the darkness shall cover me, and the light around me
>   become night,'
> even the darkness is not dark to you;
> the night is as bright as the day, for darkness is as light to you.
>   (Psalm 139:7-12)

Even though the psalmist says we cannot escape God in any way, that is good news.

The bad news is that the psalmist might be wrong. We who rush about too much live in fear that we are empty inside. If we deny ourselves long and hard enough, we can convince ourselves that we have no true self, no moral character at all, that we do not exist as personally responsible people. This is not happy Buddhist emptiness, a cleansing doctrine of no-self. It is an implosion of identity. Although God might be everywhere, we are nowhere. When we turn at last to the inward life, no one is home. Having denied it, we look frantically for our inward life of moral and religious character, and it is gone. In ultimate perspective our existence is lost. We are dead before God and ourselves, and in horror we know that we will that. This is the seriousness of sin.

With half my heart I wish you all could live in cheery oblivion of sinful offense against the inward life. I hope you approach the world so as to fix it up and suffer only mild pangs of conscience that you don't allow to accumulate as a moral character. But with the other half of my heart, I hope you can face the truth and attend to the facts of your inward life, for this is what the Christian gospel addresses.

The Letter to the Hebrews says that Jesus is a High Priest who can offer sacrifices that atone for our sins. Moreover, Jesus himself is the sacrifice, more precious than sheep or bulls, which completely redeems us. Jesus' sacrifice took place once and for all. Our sins, real as they are, no longer count against our moral character unless we hold on to them.

Now you might not like the sacrifice imagery in Hebrews, which comes from the Old Testament approach to sacrifice. But what it means for the Christian gospel is that we are accepted by God in ultimate perspective. Our moral character, sins included, is acknowledged, registered, and accepted. This is who we are, and who we are is accepted. We do not have to deny ourselves, for even the worst about us is accepted. We should have done better, but still we are accepted. We should do better in the future, but no matter what we do, we are accepted.

If we thought our souls were empty, that was a mistake because they are full of God loving us. If we thought we were dead in the inward parts, that was a mistake because God's life is there, cradling the intimate faults and virtues of our truest self. If we thought we were lost on the wings of the morning or at the farthest limits of the sea, that was a fault of our vision because, even in our flight from God, God accepts us fugitives. If we thought there was no one home in the dark night of the soul, that was a fault of our vision because God accepts even our will to be nothing. The psalmist was not wrong: not even nothingness can separate us from the love of God.

Jesus summed up the tension between God's righteousness and mercy as ever-present creative love, like a father's, and he taught his disciples to live in love with one another. Jesus' model of how to live before God as a redeemed sinner changed history. The author of the Letter to the Hebrews symbolized this with the imagery of Jesus as both the Supreme High Priest who can purify us so that we can be taken directly into God and as the sacrifice itself that makes us clean. Our purification never means denying who and what we really are. We have to be loved for ourselves or not loved at all, for God knows our inward parts. As the psalmist said: we are who we are in ultimate perspective, and that is accepted into the divine life.

The passage from Hebrews ends, "And let us consider how to provoke one another to love and good deeds, not neglecting to meet together, as is the habit of some, but encouraging one another, and all the more as you see the Day approaching." As we "see the Day approaching," which is to say that we think of ourselves in ultimate perspective, I invite you to meet together with those sinners redeemed by Christ, "to provoke one another to love and good deeds." Enter more fully into the community of friends to find courage for living life with all possible fullness, putting sin in its proper place. Sing with us to sin less in the outward ways of harming the world. Sing with us the freedom of the inward life from sin's bondage, guilt, denial, and death. Sing with us a new life made possible by the New Life in Christ whose advent we are coming to celebrate. Come sing again this song of redemption that accepts us in ultimate love and gives us personal status and eternal life before God. For when you know redemption's song deep in your heart, only then can you learn to sing the better song that lovers sing to God, our Beloved. Amen.

10

TEMPTATION IN THE WILDERNESS (A LENTEN SERMON)

Deuteronomy 26:1-11
Romans 10:8b-13
Luke 4:1-13*

IF WE HAD no temptations, we would not need Lent. Lent is a time to acknowledge our temptations, to do penance for having given in to them, and to steel ourselves with greater discipline to resist them. We do have temptations, we do give in to them, and we are too often too weak to resist them. So we do need Lent. The story of Jesus in the wilderness is a lesson in temptations.

The first thing to note is that Jesus was weakened by fasting for forty days. This might be an exaggeration of the actual time, because "forty" was a kind of biblical code for a long time—remember Noah's forty days of rain, Moses' forty days and nights on the mountain with God, and the forty years the Israelites wandered in the desert before coming to the promised land. Whatever the time Jesus actually spent in the wilderness, it was a long time and he was hungry and weak when Satan caught up with him.

The first temptation Satan put to Jesus, in Luke's account, was to offer bread in return for a little cheating, namely using divine power to turn a stone to food. Many have interpreted Luke's account to mean that Jesus

---

* Lections from the First Sunday in Lent, Year C.

had supernatural powers and could have used them but chose not to. Of course we need bread and other necessities and are tempted to take moral shortcuts to get them. We might say that in times of truly dire necessity, a little thievery is legitimate—remember *Les Misérables*; we are a merciful people. Sometimes, however, we are a bit liberal with mercy toward ourselves and justify a little cheating in studies, innocent shoplifting of ideas from the Internet, or vicious competitiveness so that we will get our own necessities. The habit of cheating grows from necessities to enhancements—better clothes, finer food, shortcuts at work to find leisure time. With the aid of a consumerist culture, we can blur the line between necessities and luxuries so that any unsatisfied desire becomes a need whose satisfaction is necessary. Step by step, we are tempted to move from cheating for self-preservation to just plain greed. We live in an Enron culture where massive cheating is taken for granted as a way of corporate life, and we are surprised when stockholders and workers are paupered by the consequences of greed. Often we don't recognize how much we participate in such a culture until some scandal suddenly turns the lights on. Note that Jesus had nothing negative to say about bread, or even riches, per se; he said only that we do not live by them alone and, when we do, they hold us in bondage, as they did the winsome but rich young ruler who asked Jesus about eternal life. Thank God we have Lent to think these things through, repent, and do better.

Satan's second temptation was power, which Jesus could have gained by worshiping the devil, that is, the spirit of destruction and control that was contrary to the God of creativity. If we have power, of course, we are able to get the necessities and even luxuries of life. As Faust knew, with power we can do great social good. Yet power brings more than the satisfaction of greed. Power evokes respect—glory, Satan said—and it gives control. Although there are some things we should control, the desire for control is an infinite passion. It has no natural satisfaction. Jesus declined Satan's power and said you should worship only God. The clue, in the story, to detecting power as a temptation is that worldly power was Satan's to give in the first place. Jesus' response indicates that its pursuit is idolatrous. Are our fantasies about power really ways of worshiping ourselves as if we were God? Our nation has so much power now that patriotism borders on idolatry. The motivation alleged for our greed is the virtue of global capitalism in a form that benefits us before it does the developing countries. The motivation alleged for our pre-emptive wars of self-defense is panic over possible weapons of mass destruction. Yet these motivations, even coupled together and accepted as valid, seem insufficient to explain our recent national exercises of power. Is display of power for its own sake the motive? Thank God we have Lent to think these things over, to repent, and amend our ways.

The third temptation was for Jesus to jump from the Temple's tower to prove that he was under divine protection. He declined, saying that God should not be put to the test. We rarely have such dramatic temptations. Nevertheless many of us, perhaps all of us sometimes, conceive God to have an obligation to take care of us in worldly matters, and we become angry, or depressed, or lose our faith when luck and nature take their mindless course. If you jump from a high place, you fall: that's the way God made gravity. If you contract a germ you get sick: that's the way God made life. If your loved one leaves you, your heart breaks: that's the way God made freedom and the human heart. To expect God to work miracles setting aside the way creation works is to "test" God, to use Jesus language. Have we tested God and been disappointed so as to corrode our faith? "Do not put the Lord your God to the test," said Jesus. Thank God we have Lent to think these things over, repent, and amend our ways.

Temptation is a creeping phenomenon. Remember the old prayer of confession? "We have erred and strayed from thy ways like lost sheep." With our eyes down on the grass in front of us, intending no evil, we follow the green rather than the proper path and get lost. "We have followed too much the devices and desires of our own hearts." Well, of course, being lost from the community with its good shepherd we are left to our own devices. "We have offended against thy holy laws." That's what comes from too much dependence on the devices and desires of our own hearts, and suddenly we are seriously culpable for moral misdeeds. "We have left undone those things which we ought to have done." So much for duty. "And we have done those things which we ought not to have done." Serious transgressions are our responsibility. "And there is no health in us." We have succumbed so far into temptation, a sickness unto death, that we have no power to stop the fall. Even though we start with small, forgivable temptations, we plummet until we are bound to endless greed, power, and self-glorification, powerless to stop.

Now we can see the special temptation in the Grand Inquisitor's conversation with Christ in Dostoyevsky's *The Brothers Karamazov.* The Grand Inquisitor—during the fifteenth-century Spanish Inquisition—chastises Jesus for wanting to make people free. People are weak and in bondage to sin, the Inquisitor said. They do not want freedom and responsibility.

They want bread as a magic handout, they want some power to take care of them with proper pomp and glory, and they want a divine guarantee that everything will be all right. Because people are like sheep, they should be treated like sheep. Because they have in fact succumbed to the temptations, the devil is in charge, and a proper religion should go along with the Grand Inquisitor's authoritarian ways that provide for everything: not to do so would be cruel. Jesus was not convinced. How many of us believe, or hope, that God will take care of everything? God is not the one who "takes care of everything." That's Satan. God makes us free.

Think back on the story of Jesus' temptation in the wilderness. Jesus had just been baptized, and the text says he was "full of the Holy Spirit." The Spirit, not chance, led him in the wilderness. It was an act of God that he be tempted. One of the ironies about Satan here and in other biblical passages is that, although he is a troublemaker and a genuinely evil spirit, he is also the witting or unwitting agent of God. To be tempted is part of the created life that we have. If we were not tempted, we would not be alive in a human way. Temptations are tests to prepare us for serious work, as Jesus was about to undertake.

Please do not mis-hear me on this point. I do not mean to say, nor does the Bible, that we should seek out temptations as a kind of spiritual discipline. That is a sure road to disaster. Only someone already besotted by the sin of pride would deliberately seek out temptations so as to exercise the ability to put them aside. In the King James version, Jesus says "Lead us not into temptation, but deliver us from evil." Let us escape as many temptations as we can: more than enough will confront us anyway, for they are part of life.

Life for us all tempts us to panic about possessing things. Even when possessions are necessities of life, they should not define life for us. Jesus was very hungry, but he did not need bread: he was deliberately fasting. Precisely because hunger and desire are natural, they will tempt us to give them misplaced importance. Our very freedom to live before God as responsible in ultimate perspective requires that we face, and face down, such temptations.

Life as such leads us to seek power, for how else can we carry out responsibilities? Yet the acquisition of power is so seductive that we can pursue it beyond measure—never enough power! We honor and glorify our little power supplies, and soon we are worshiping not God but ourselves. Actually, it is not ourselves that we worship. People who succumb to the need for power, paradoxically, are internally weak and need the power to give themselves substance and identity. Rather, we worship the sources of power: as Satan said, Jesus could have all power and authority to do good if only he would worship Satan who had the power and authority to give. Like most people seduced by Satan, we think we do it for ourselves when in fact we are serving a hidden master. Because the hidden master is the promise of power without regard for direction and measure, it is a chaos of blind forces, an unleashing of mindless spirits. If seduction by possessions leads to a panic of desire, seduction by power leads a pandemonium of powers beyond our control.

Life as such presents endless occasions to test God's goodness and to demand it. A deep paradox lies in the fact that because every bit of life comes from God, our gratitude for life itself should be infinite. At the same time, with life come also the dangers, shortcomings, sufferings, and death that are as much a part as the beauty, love, opportunities, health, and new beginnings. If our idea of God is small, we expect God to run the world as our ideal parents would, with constant provision for every need and defense against every threat. Should our parents give us a stone instead of bread, we would say they don't love us. To think that way is to test God. If our idea of God is as immense as Jesus', however, we know that the grace of creation is enough, even with its dangers, pains, and death. The immense God's love is proved in the Christ who teaches us to embrace the suffering and death in life as the way properly to embrace the divine immensity. Although we cannot help being tempted to test God with a demand for proof of love, we can nevertheless follow Jesus in setting that temptation aside. Maturity means that we take responsibility for engaging life as it comes, not as we wish God would make it.

I have two final points. First, when Jesus met Satan in the wilderness, he knew something was up. For us, temptations come more subtly, like greener grass to grazing sheep and then before we know it we are enslaved to greed and power and angry with the God who we think has not done enough for us lately. Be careful.

Second, although Jesus' fasting might have made him hungry and weak in a physical sense, it made him strong in a spiritual sense, strong enough to withstand the temptation to become the kind of false messiah his people, his friends, and Dostoyevsky's Grand Inquisitor wanted. Although our Lenten fasting is a pale imitation of Jesus' wilderness discipline, it is a strong help as we engage the life of temptation in order to love the God who gives it. May Lent be a proper wilderness for us all.

I pray then for a wilderness of life to expose our civilized cover-ups. Let us be as sheep without a shepherd who have to be alert to their own stray-ings—then we can give ourselves to a Shepherd who demands that we be free. I pray for a wilderness in which the devices and desires of our own hearts become fully known to us—then we can be free to bring them to perfection. I pray for a wilderness where God's right is starkly before us—then, like Jesus, we can will the right or the fall with our own free souls. I pray for a wilderness where no sophistications becloud our doing what we ought and not doing what we ought not—then we can present our-selves to the One who calls us as disciples ready for instruction. I pray for a wilderness in which our sickness unto death is revealed and healed in fasting and penance—then we can give our whole heart, mind, soul, and strength to the One who leads us through death to resurrection.

Church, we have entered into the Lenten Season as into a wilderness. May our temptations be seen as clearly as Jesus saw Satan and our responses be as faithful as Jesus' own resolution. Amen.

11.

NOT MANY SHOULD
BECOME TEACHERS

Proverbs 1:20-33
James 3:1-12
Mark 8:27-38*

THE TEXTS FOR this sermon are enough to give one pause about a
university pulpit. The passage from Proverbs 1 starts happily
enough with a strong speech by Dame Wisdom, one of the Bible's
most outrageous characters, who begins "How long, O simple ones, will
you love being simple?" She goes on to say that she pours out her
thoughts but the simple ones ignore them, leading to their calamity. "For
waywardness kills the simple, and the complacency of fools destroys
them." What an advertisement for higher education!

It is dangerous to be simple. The philosopher Alfred North Whitehead
said that we should seek simplicity, but distrust it. He was right. The reason to distrust simplicity is the narrowness of evidence it takes into
account. Unless simplicity is a state of mind and soul attained after mas-
tering worlds of complexity—and this is not what Dame Wisdom had in
mind—it lives on inherited prejudices for which a person can barely be
responsible. Simple people of the sort Dame Wisdom criticized are ignorant of cultures different from their own and of circumstances where
things are at stake that are different from the issues of their own circumstances. This often makes them bigots with regard to different people,
fools with regard to different circumstances, and complacent when some
new beast comes slouching toward their holy place. The world today does

---

* Lections for Proper 19, Sunday between September 11 and September 17, Year B.

not allow many people to meet only their own kind or deal only with their inherited circumstances. The university at its best sometimes imparts the vision and experience required for wisdom. A university pulpit should aspire to this task in religious matters.

Nevertheless, a great gulf exists between Dame Wisdom, the divine personage of the Book of Proverbs, and us mortal teachers. The university finds it easy to miss the mark in the wisdom department and should take to heart the admonition in the Letter of James with which I title this sermon: "Not many of you should become teachers, my brothers and sisters, for you know that we who teach will be judged with greater strictness. For all of us make many mistakes." James went on to say that the tongue of a teacher is like a bridle on a horse, a rudder in a ship, or a little fire in a tinder forest—small but capable of enormous consequences. We so-called teachers of wisdom need humility, James warned.

Perhaps James had in mind the incident related in our text from Mark's Gospel. The disciples were abuzz because people were saying that Jesus was John the Baptist or Elijah or some other prophet come back from the dead. Jesus asked Peter what he thought, and Peter answered that Jesus was the Messiah. In Matthew's account of this incident, Jesus says that God must have revealed this to Peter because Peter's "flesh and blood" was not bright enough to get it. Immediately after this Jesus said that he, Jesus, would be made to suffer, would be rejected, killed, and then would rise in three days. Peter, back in the flesh and blood mode, rebuked Jesus for saying these horrible depressing things. Jesus retorted to his prize student, "Get behind me, Satan! For you are setting your mind not on divine things but on human things." Given Peter's subsequent role in the Christian movement, we have a super object-lesson of teachers getting it wrong. Teachers can go from true witness to unwitting Satanic betrayal without batting an eye. Peter thought he was just cheering up Jesus when he got wrong the whole meaning of Jesus' identity as Messiah.

Religious teachers have a difficult road to walk, responding to Wisdom's demand to help the simple without making some small mistake, often out of a desire to comfort, that has very large and damning consequences. If the only teachers in question were preachers and professors, this point would have a valid but limited range of application. The problem is that we all are religious teachers for our neighbors, children, and friends. James might well have written, "Not many should become teachers, but for better or worse you all will be."

Therefore we should look more carefully at what Jesus said went wrong with Peter: "You are setting your mind not on divine things but on human things." What can this mean? Perhaps it depends on the audience. Mark is particularly detailed in his account of who was talking to whom in this incident. Jesus asked his small group of disciples about his identity, and in that intimate group Peter said Jesus was the Messiah; Jesus responded by enjoining the disciples not to tell anyone else about this identification and then explained to them that he would suffer, die, and be raised. Peter took Jesus aside in private to rebuke him, but Jesus turned back to the whole group of disciples to rebuke Peter as Satan: he did not respond to Peter alone, as he might have if he were gently correcting his favorite student. He meant it as a lesson for the disciples. Then Jesus immediately called the large crowd of followers to join the disciples and made the remarkable speech about how they would have to deny themselves and take up their cross in order to follow him. "For those who want to save their life will lose it, and those who lose their life for my sake and for the sake of the gospel, will save it."

In Mark's text, Jesus' address to the crowd is an interpretation of setting your mind on divine rather than human things. The crowd did not know that Jesus was the Messiah. They did not know that the Messiah was to be betrayed, killed, and raised from the dead, a point that only the disciples had heard and had not yet comprehended. What the crowd was told was that following Jesus is a matter of life and death.

In Deuteronomy 30, Moses had told the Israelites, as they were about to enter the promised land, that he set before them life and death: choose life, that you might live, he said. Jesus renewed that challenge but with a huge twist. Moses said that to choose life, which meant following God's commandments, would secure long life and prosperity in the promised land. Jesus said that to choose life, which meant following him and his gospel, could lead to forfeiting both worldly success and life. Those who would save their life in Moses' sense of gaining the world will lose it. Those who lose their lives to follow Jesus will gain it in a divine sense.

Jesus' main point is at the heart of the Christian gospel, and it has two sides.

First, in the divine perspective, right living before God does not correlate with worldly success. To be good does not necessarily lead to long life and prosperity. As we would put it, there is no divine moral governance of the world, rewarding the worthy and punishing the wicked. Rather, Jesus' paradigm is that the Messiah who restores people to a right relation to God gets betrayed and killed. Resurrection for Jesus did not mean that he would return with an army to drive out the Romans and establish justice, nor did it mean that he would return to set up a university that surpassed Plato's and Aristotle's in teaching divinity. In the most literal reading of the resurrection accounts, Jesus left the earth for heaven after forty days. History remained ambiguous and treacherous for Christians ever after. So we should not expect the ordinary life of even the saints among us to be more successful in worldly senses than education, prudence, and luck can make them. Nor is suffering a mark of divine disfavor, however much most of the world's religions, including corrupt forms of Christianity, have believed that.

Second, the gospel is that the true meaning of life is to be found in the ultimate perspective of God. Jesus had a lot to say about this, including the readiness to deny ourselves for others, to build communities of love, and to witness to the divine perspective when the world has other values. Next week the gospel text is about how those who would be first will be last, and vice versa. The central task of Christian teachers—and all Christians teach one way or another—is to articulate what life looks like from the ultimate perspective of God, what its ultimate predicaments are in contrast to its worldly problems, and what its ultimate salvation consists in contrasted with the lure of worldly successes.

In pre-classical times many people believed in God as a kind of superhuman agent, with human virtues and powers intensified to a supernatural degree. With this conception, the divine perspective was something like an all-powerful control panel for history. God could be imagined as a totally righteous and powerful king insuring justice within history. In classical times, including the time of Jesus, many people believed in God as an infinitely removed Spirit high above a cosmic stack of heavens and hells, and they believed that souls were immortal or, as in the Christian case, could be raised whole with a celestial body. The classical conception imagined the divine perspective as placing a soul after death in a level of heaven or hell appropriate to the person's merit; for Pauline Christianity it meant that because of Jesus' merit the saved went to the highest heaven where Jesus in a properly celestial form dwelt with God the Father. Some among us might share these pre-classical and classical assumptions, both of which are found in the Bible. But many of us read the Bible and imagine God differently. Our task as teachers today is to articulate the ultimacy of the divine perspective and its significance for what is ultimately important in human life, for a world understood through modern science, shaped by confrontations of civilizations and criticized by the prophets of imagination.

I invite you all to take seriously what it means to be a follower of Rabbi Jesus. Have pity on the simple people of the world, teach them the complexities of life, and strive for a new simplicity while distrusting it. Join with the disciples in learning that the most Satanic simplicity is to judge ultimate matters with worldly standards. Hear with the crowd that the choice of ultimately true life in following Jesus is costly in worldly terms. Please join with those who would deny themselves the ambition to gain the world and enter into the discipline required to teach divine wisdom to the simple. For the simple will be taught by us no matter what we do. I invite you into the Christian Way in which we catch a glimpse of divine wisdom through living a life patterned by crucifixion and resurrection, as Jesus told the simple disciples. Amen.

12.

WHILE THE LORD MAY BE FOUND (A LENTEN SERMON)

Isaiah 55:1-9
1 Corinthians 10:1-13
*Luke 13:1-9**

OUR TEXT FROM Isaiah is uncommonly cheery for Lent. Yet it is at the heart of Lent's meaning. "Ho, everyone who thirsts, come to the waters; and you that have no money, come, buy and eat! Come, buy wine and milk without money and without price. Why do you spend your money for that which is not bread and your labor for that which does not satisfy? Listen carefully to me, and eat what is good, and delight yourselves in rich food." Two thousand five hundred years before the Atkins diet, the Jews knew that rich food is the stuff of divine favor. Milk, honey, wine, oil, fresh water, bread, and fatted calves advertised fulfillment in the promised land.

These viands were cited metaphorically, of course, to give content to God's promise. But they worked as metaphors because they also were literally among the blessings of a prosperous and happy people. Knowing what we do today about alcohol, cholesterol, and the effects of too much fat, we might officially prefer the metaphoric to the literal meaning. But if we can imagine heaven as filled with pleasures that have no bad consequences, deep in our hearts we would want to dine on richly marbled hotel-cut roast beef with béarnaise sauce, followed by crème

---

* Lections for the Third Sunday in Lent, Year C.

73

brûlée, then chocolate truffles and baklava; cigars would be nice for the gentlemen. How I regret that this Victorian appetite was so unhealthy, sexist, and funded by the labors of others, usually conquered peoples! People in the ancient world did not have these hygienic and moral concerns about the good life.

Our text from Isaiah concludes a section that began with chapter 40 and that was written probably in the second half of the sixth century BCE while the Jewish elite was exiled in Babylon. The first thirty-nine chapters of Isaiah, which scholars call First Isaiah, were written in the second half of the eighth century BCE by someone who really was named Isaiah, the son of Amoz. The Assyrians had conquered the Northern Kingdom of Israel in the time of First Isaiah, and the Babylonians had conquered the Southern Kingdom of Judah a few decades before the writing of our text. Chapters 56 to 66, Third Isaiah, were written toward the end of the sixth century after the exiles had returned to Jerusalem. Our text is the culmination of Second Isaiah, celebrating the exiles' anticipation that Cyrus of Persia, who had conquered the Babylonians, would send the exiles home. Cyrus did send them home and for that was called a messiah. The Jews in the sixth century were overjoyed to be going home, returning to the promised land, a second exodus from a second exile. Chapter 55 concludes after our reading by saying "For you shall go out in joy, and be led back in peace; the mountains and the hills before you shall burst into song, and all the trees of the field shall clap their hands. Instead of the thorn shall come up the cypress; instead of the brier shall come up the myrtle; and it shall be to the LORD for a memorial, for an everlasting sign that shall not be cut off."

Isaiah was one of the most important sources of images for early Christian self-understanding. Our passage resonates with Jesus' claim, recorded in John's Gospel, to be the water of life to which the thirsty should come, the bread of life for those who are hungry. Part of the very deep resonances in the Eucharistic elements of bread and wine is that, while they symbolize the broken body and spilled blood of Jesus, they also are the biblical signs of prosperity and happiness. Although part of the assertion of the early Christians that Jesus was the Messiah came from tracing his genealogy through his father, Joseph, back to King David (the second messiah, after King Saul), another part came from analogy with Cyrus, the messiah who set the Jewish people free.

The early Christians, however, transformed the meanings of these symbols as they applied them to Jesus. They had to do so. Our text from Isaiah makes reference to God's promise to establish the House of David on the throne of Israel forever, and that simply did not happen. The Isaiah text speaks as if the whole nation of Israel has a messianic role, when in fact it became fragmented. Whereas most of the other Jewish sects at the time of the Second Temple waited for a new messiah like David, or perhaps a Roman Cyrus, the Christians, who were then one more Jewish sect, changed the whole meaning of messiahship and many other Jewish symbols. The other Jews sought a messiah who would establish Israel in the land and perhaps make Jerusalem the world's capital. The Christians came to believe that the religious problem has little to do with settling in the land. It has to do rather with settling in God. We are estranged from God, like Israelites who have broken the covenant. The Messiah is the one who overcomes our estrangement. The question for us in our day is how to understand this God and our estrangement.

The Isaiah text contains this wonderful line: "For my thoughts are not your thoughts, nor are your ways my ways, says the LORD. For as the heavens are higher than the earth, so are my ways higher than your ways and my thoughts than your thoughts." This is a highly anthropomorphic representation of God speaking. Astonishingly, what God says is that the anthropomorphic representations do not apply. God is not just a smarter, deeper thinker. God does not think in the sense that we do. God is as different as the heaven is higher than the earth. This theme runs throughout Second Isaiah, which is one of the earliest biblical books to say that God is the Creator of absolutely everything, not just the heavenly king and defender of Israel, but Creator of everything and Lord of all nations.

In our time, the conception of God as Creator must accommodate a vastly enriched conception of the "everything" created. The universe is 15 to 20 billion years old and vaster in extent than we can imagine; it is not the small, earth-centered cosmos imagined in the first century. We understand the peoples of the world to be not only those of the Mediterranean basin, nor even those of all the earth; God is Creator of whatever rational desirous beings there are throughout the billions of galaxies, each with its own history, perhaps of sin and redemption. We understand the differences between subjective mind and objective reality, between inner personality and outer social roles, between temporal endurance and spatial location, all to be created differences. The fundamental physical and metaphysical characteristics of the world are themselves created. The Creator, then, cannot be a mind over against a world to be known, not a person interacting with individuals or peoples, not a temporal entity lasting throughout all time, or located in one place or all places. Those are all creaturely traits and can be ascribed to God only metaphorically. Because we now know something of the immensity of creation, we know that God the Creator is immense. We are humbled by the difficulty of grasping the immense God in concepts derived from creation. We know that to ascribe to God characteristics that would make God a creature is idolatry. So we keep perfecting our symbols of God and then break them to keep them from idolatry.

One thing we do know, however, is that, as creatures, we are the actualized completion, the conclusions, the finish, the termini, of the divine creative act. God does not create us and then let us go: because space and time are as much creatures as we, no spatio-temporal medium exists apart from God into which we could be put. Nothing is outside of God. God's creative act is the constituting of space-time and everything in it, in all their interwoven connections. *What* we are, God creates. *That* we are, is God's living creative act itself, with us as the completion of the act, the breaking of the wave whose surge has crossed an infinite sea. We are the dance of the divine dancer, the song of the divine singer. God is the Creator of the cosmos, and we are God's creative act as it is realized. At whatever time we are, that is God making us then. Wherever we are, that is God making us there. In all our connections to the environment, with each other, with the histories of our peoples, of the earth, with the stars of heaven—that is God creating this network of creatures playing out their lives in space and time. No creature can be separate from God, for to be at all is to be a local part of the immense act of divine creation.

Because we are so local, however, we easily forget both our connections with others throughout this cosmos and our roots in God's creativity. We become selfish. And then we notice that the cosmos fills our life with griefs as well as joys, suffering as well as rich food, persecutions as well as support, and with lives always short according to the cosmic calendar. So perversely we organize ourselves in rejection of the divine ground of our being. Instead of gratitude we feel anger, instead of bright attention we cultivate anaesthesia, instead of joyous humility we define ourselves by pride. We think we deserve bounty. We sell our souls to the promise of power to control our lives. We imagine the immense God to be a mere supernatural person whose good will we test and usually find wanting. In sum, we are estranged, despite the fact our very existence is the shining forth of God's creative act. This is quite different from literally being exiled outside of the promised land.

Or is it? The promised land for Christians is life in God's creative act from which we cannot be removed even when we think we are. To be estranged is to be in denial about our own very existence, which we can see now to be the work of love in divine creativity. To be reconciled is not to be moved from outside God into the divine heart. It is to be turned to recognize where we already are, beloved with one another by the Creator giving us being, steadied in the divine promises that give us life however ambiguous. The Messiah who turns us to accept our Creator and ourselves as creatures is not a military king who wins land for us. It is the one who shows us how to live in gratitude for our lives within the divine life. It is the one who leads us to endure the sufferings of life so as to be at one with the fullness of life in God. It is the one who creates for us communities of shared love in which we can mature as lovers of one another and of our creator. Christians proclaim that Jesus is this Messiah.

Let us then read Isaiah with a Christian revision of his symbols. "Seek the LORD while he may be found, call upon him while he is near." Our Creator is always here, within us and our fellows, in our mountains, rivers, seas, plains, forests, fields, highways, houses, buildings, schools, factories, hospitals, ghettos, battlefields, starvation, poverty, depression, hate, war, sickness, and death. God is never absent. Jesus says to turn and seek God in all these things. Nothing in life is beyond bearing if we bear it resting on the divine pulse of creativity. Life is ambiguous and fragmentary. Its complexities are nuanced beyond imagination, and we grasp but its surface. Nevertheless, when Jesus turns us to God, our gratitude and love can embrace the whole of God's gift.

We know in this life that it is better to be full than hungry, satisfied than thirsty, rich than poor, healthy than sick, alive than dead. All these good things are worth pursuing. Nevertheless Jesus taught that there is a different kind of hunger and thirst, wealth and health, indeed life itself, than these relative things. When we are estranged, it's hard to recognize the hunger and thirst for God; it's hard to distinguish true wealth from mere riches, true health from a gym body, true life from more ordinary life. When we see the God in Jesus, however, our true hunger and thirst are made plain. The gospel for Lent is that the hunger and thirst for God can be satisfied by God our intimate Creator. The abundance of the entire creation is our wealth, the wholeness of the cosmos is our health, the life of the Creator is our life. God's everlasting covenant with us is that if we but turn to our Creator, God, who, as Augustine said, has always been nearer to us than we are to ourselves, will be accessible to satisfy our hunger and thirst.

Let us now use our Lenten discipline to put down our relative hungers and thirsts and desires for wealth, health, and longevity. Instead let us stoke to fever pitch our hunger and thirst for God, our longing for God's abundance and vibrancy and true life. We long for these too little and need more passion for them, an infinite passion. For the good news is that God says: "Ho, everyone who thirsts, come to the waters; and you that have no money, come, buy and eat! Come, buy wine and milk without money and without price. Why do you spend your money for that which is not bread, and your labor for that which does not satisfy? Listen carefully to me, and eat what is good, and delight yourselves in rich food. Incline your ear, and come to me; listen, so that you may live. I will make with you an everlasting covenant." Amen.

13.

LIFE FROM DEATH
(AN EASTER SERMON)

John 20:1-18
Luke 24:1-12*

A LLELUIA, CHRIST IS risen! He is risen indeed! This is the central affirmation of Christianity. Its metaphoric sweep is broader and deeper than any specifics about Jesus. Concerning what they believe happened to Jesus, Christians contradict one another in many ways. Many Christians simply don't care much about the specifics of Jesus. And yet all agree that the meaning of Easter is that new life comes from the bleakest of circumstances, even death, and that this new life is available to us, our hope. If Easter were only about Jesus and not about our own hope, it would not be so central to Christianity.

The metaphoric sweep of life from death encompasses far more even than Christianity and is symbolized in other ways than Jesus' resurrection. All the great and small religions in climatic zones with distinct changes of seasons celebrate the new life of spring emerging from the death of winter. Some religions focus on the celebration of the season itself. Others celebrate founding events in the springtime, such as Passover. Ancient paganism celebrated the dying and rising of gods. Our late-modern urbanized societies are less close to the land, less immediately conscious of the spring thaw making our livelihood possible. Yet even in Boston where I live, prayers for the coming of spring after a hard winter are second only to prayers for the Red Sox. More than that, in Boston, hope for the Red Sox's new season is our central sacrament in the pan-religious celebration of new life from death.

---

* Lections for Easter Day, Year C.

Because we have hope that new life can come from death, we have hope even when people we love have died, we have hope in the face of illness, we have hope for careers despite failures, we have hope to improve spiritually, we have hope to gain health, to build strength, to lose weight, to slow aging, we have hope for our families, for our friends, for our enemies, we have hope to improve our neighborhoods, our schools, our local governments, we have hope to conquer racism, we have hope to lessen poverty, we have hope to respect our environment, we have hope for courage to engage our time, we have hope to overturn prejudice against ethnic and gender minorities, we have hope to ban unfair discrimination from our laws, we have hope to understand cultures that are threatened by our own, we have hope for peace in central Africa, Palestine, and Northern Ireland, we have hope that the peoples of Afghanistan and Iraq will soon govern themselves, we have hope to remove the grounds for terrorism and to stop the terrorists, we have hope to stop making war, we have hope for the justice of our economy, we have hope for the honesty of our government—and in Boston, we have hope that the Red Sox will win the World Series (again) this year! It is a metaphysical condition of the cosmos at our scale of things that new life is possible in the worst of conditions, even death or the Yankees.

I heartily welcome all of you, not because you may be dedicated to the community of Jesus but because you are celebrating spring, the resurrection of life from death, and the ever-recurrent hope that our intractable griefs and obstacles can be overcome. When Martin Luther King Jr., said "I have a dream that someday . . ." he was expressing his bigger-than-Easter faith. Christianity is but one way of symbolizing that hope which defines the human spirit under pressure.

Let me turn now, however, to the specifically Christian way of having that faith and hope. Christianity is based on the cosmic drama of creation and redemption. I have been preaching through Lent on the vastness of creation and how to understand that in terms of our own knowledge now. Whatever else might happen in the rest of the cosmos, on Earth human beings have become faulty creatures, symbolized by the Fall. Human faults are of many kinds, and I listed some of them in respect of which we have hope for repair. The chief fault, however, is that people are estranged from God the Creator who gives them a world filled with joys and troubles. The proper relation to God was symbolized by the covenant between God and Israel, according to which those who are pure and holy in terms of the covenant can approach God. That was symbolized as approaching the Holy of Holies where God is. Alas, people constantly break the covenant and as a result cannot approach God. As a restorative remedy, the Torah, particularly the book of Leviticus, specifies sacrifices that people can have made on their behalf by the priests to repair specific breaches of the covenant, thereby restoring their readiness to approach God.

In Jesus' time, however, the system of Temple sacrifices to enable a proper relation to God was widely perceived as not working. For one thing, out of political necessity to keep the Temple functioning those who managed the Temple had to be collaborators with the Roman Empire. The Sadducees, mentioned in the Gospels, were the "party" associated with the Temple, and their collaboration with Pontius Pilate in the trial of Jesus illustrates what was probably a widespread political reality. Many people felt that under these circumstances the practice of the religion of Israel had become lax and corrupt. Some extreme groups, such as the Essenes, attempted to live apart from the larger society altogether. Preachers such as John the Baptist and Jesus began reform movements within the larger society, preaching repentance and a purer practice of the relation to God. The Pharisees were a group or movement that supplemented worship in the Temple with a quasi-independent religious life centered in local synagogues, advocating earnestness about keeping the law and a personal piety centered in the family. When the Temple was destroyed a generation after Jesus, the Pharisaic movement, loosely defined, became the default center of Judaism because it could flourish without the Temple, though always remembering it. What we know as Judaism today is descended from the Pharisees and associated reform movements within Second Temple Judaism. Jesus' own teaching was within the general orbit of the Pharisaical reform movement, contrary to the impression you might get from the Gospels that depict the Pharisees as debate partners with Jesus; it was something of an in-house debate.

Jesus preached not only a critical message, as seems to have been the case with John the Baptist, but also a very hopeful message. His followers had great expectations on Palm Sunday and were devastated by his death on Friday. When the tomb was reported empty on Sunday, the disciples suddenly paid attention to some of the strange things Jesus had taught, hard lessons they had refused to understand, such as that the first shall be last and the last first, that it's easier to relate to God if you are a loser than if you are a winner, and that he himself would be killed and rise again. Then the disciples began seeing Jesus here and there. Many of the post-resurrection appearances of Jesus are strange. Often his close disciples don't recognize him at first, as Mary Magdalene in our Gospel mistook Jesus for a gardener, or the people on the road to Emmaus walked with a man most of the day before recognizing him as Jesus when he broke the bread at dinner. I don't know whether you think that Jesus' resurrection means his corpse was resuscitated, a point that has been debated for centuries. Some people would say that Mary mistook a real gardener for Jesus. I myself do not believe the issue is important because the disciples found the person of Jesus in whomever they saw and believed to be Jesus. The theologian Robert A. Jensen says that Jesus' resurrected body is wherever his person is to be found, which is why we can say that the communion elements are the body of Christ or that the church is the body of Christ. The point is, Jesus lived again for the disciples and later for Paul, and they were profoundly transformed by that. How so?

Remember in our Gospel text Jesus tells Mary Magdalene not to touch him because he had not yet ascended to God but was about to do so. The early church's profound transformation came with its understanding of the ascension. Think what it means. First, the ascension means the possibility of approaching God without the Temple. Second, Jesus himself was able to approach God that way. The Letter to the Hebrews calls Jesus our High Priest who goes into the heavenly Holy of Holies for us. Third, Jesus goes to prepare a place for the disciples so they, too, can approach God. Fourth, Jesus sends the Holy Spirit so the disciples can live in right relation to God in the midst of their struggles in ordinary life. This in effect is a total restoration of the covenant, and Jesus' death symbolically is the sacrifice to end all sacrifices. Its importance is not to appease an angry God but to perfect and transform the covenant relation of Israel to God. Within twenty years of the beginning of the Christian movement, the apostle Paul generalized this point to say that Jesus made it possible for Gentiles, not only Jews, to inherit the covenant promises made to Israel. Jesus makes God cosmically accessible to everyone, and the Holy Spirit helps us live in right relation to all that.

Understanding this, the first disciples were transformed from what Paul called "old beings" living under the broken covenant to "new beings" who were rightly related to God. Jesus had taught that the right relation was to love God with all your heart, mind, soul, and strength, and your neighbor as yourself. Participation in the new covenant, extending the old, is to be a lover of God and neighbor. The idea of becoming a lover is easily generalizable, like new life from death; in fact, becoming a lover *is* new life from death.

So the early Christians cultivated loving communities as well as devotion to the love of God. What does it mean to love your neighbor? It means to be kind in all ways. But more important, it means to help your neighbor become a better lover, a new being. Thus began the particular history of the development of Christian communities around the globe and down through history to us. Its glory is that the resurrected Christ is seen in the persons of the saints, in our sacraments, teachings, good works, and in the church itself as the body of Christ. Its shame is that our Christian communities have so often failed to embody Christ. For both cases, the risen and ascended Christ is judge over the church, accessible through the Holy Spirit in our imaginations and discriminated by our minds in careful discernment of spirits. For nearly two thousand years, Jesus has lived in the church's imagination and grown as Lord of the church, creating lovers and reconciling people to God, addressing issues the young Galilean could never have imagined before the resurrection.

The good news is that there is a power abroad in the churches that makes new beings of us, that makes us God-lovers and lovers of one another. Loving God and one another, we can face death as the price of life. We can engage the vital and sometimes intractable issues of our watch with genuine hope. That power is the person of Jesus raised from the dead into countless bodies around us, lovers all, ascended into heaven as our eternal host in God, king of the universe who makes possible our life before God, historical pioneer and perfecter of the Christian movement, the dear friend who can live in our hearts, the Savior who embraces the worst of us, and when we fall again, embraces us again, the Way to come to God, the Truth of God's justice and mercy, the Life whose substance is love. These symbols of Jesus are the Christian's ways to engage God in gratitude for the creation, in humility before the Creator, and in love that embraces all the Creator's creation. If only in part, we have felt this gratitude, we have knelt in humility, we have loved this love. I tell you, like the disciples waking up at Emmaus, in this we have seen the Risen Christ! Alleluia! Christ is risen! He is risen indeed! Amen.

CALL

14.

THE LAST BREAKFAST

Acts 9:1-6 (7-20)
Revelation 5:11-14
John 21:1-19*

WE ARE ACCUSTOMED to giving much attention to the Last Supper, the meal Jesus had with his disciples the night in which he was betrayed and on which we base the Eucharist. The Gospel of John, however, in its account of the Last Supper does not include the Eucharistic words of institution, Jesus' admonition to take the bread and wine as his body and blood. John cites Jesus saying these words much earlier in his ministry with the very strong claim that those who do not eat his body and drink his blood have no share in eternal life (John 6). In John's version of the Last Supper, the ritual activity is foot washing.

In contrast to the other Gospels, John's ends with a long and intricate epilogue in which the resurrected Jesus appears to a select and mostly named group of disciples in Galilee and cooks them breakfast. Some scholars believe that the last chapter of John is a late addition, mainly because it differs so much from the other Gospel accounts. If it is a late addition, which I doubt, it still expresses the most important distinctive themes of John's Gospel and is a kind of balancing text to the famous prologue, "In the beginning was the Word, and the Word was with God, and the Word was God."

One of John's distinctive approaches throughout his Gospel is the use of symbolic allegory. So, for instance, Jesus feeds the disciples breakfast and then tells Simon Peter, their leader, to feed his sheep, meaning all the others whom Jesus loves. Jesus' breakfast is an allegorical act defining the

---

* Lections for the Third Sunday of Easter, Year C.

work of the church. We take the sheep to refer to us, although I don't know how you like being thought of as sheep.

Another of John's distinctive approaches is seemingly the opposite of high allegory, namely an attention to details. For instance, in the breakfast scene he names the disciples: Peter, Thomas, Nathanael, the sons of Zebedee, and two others, one of whom is likely the Beloved Disciple whose testimony is the basis for the Gospel of John. John puts in the detail about Peter getting so excited and confused when he realizes that Jesus is on the shore that he puts on his clothes and then jumps overboard to swim back to Jesus. I love the detail that they caught 153 fish. Which one of the disciples do you suppose counted them?

Perhaps the most important detail is that Jesus is personally concerned about the disciples. The first thing Jesus says to them is, "Lads, you have no fish, have you?" When they report that he is right, he tells them where to cast the net, and they haul in 153. Struggling to shore with the laden boat, they find that Jesus has already brought bread, laid a charcoal fire, caught some fish himself, and is cooking the fish for them. He asks them to come eat the breakfast. Yet apparently they hang back. John says "None of the disciples dared to ask him, 'Who are you?'" Somehow they knew it was Jesus, yet it must not have looked like him. This problem of recognition is like the first resurrection appearance that John records, when Mary Magdalene first thinks Jesus is the gardener. In the two other resurrection appearances in John's Gospel (there are four in all), Jesus looks like himself with the wounds of his crucifixion. However we are to understand the resurrection appearances, following the theologian Robert A. Jensen, the real body of the resurrected Jesus is wherever the person of Jesus is present to us. The person of Jesus was calling them to breakfast. "Jesus came and took the bread and gave it to them, and did the same with the fish." He served them to allay their fear and wonder. He cared for them with a touching intimacy, tender with their confusions.

Remember that at the Last Supper he had washed the disciples' feet, another intimate touch, and then had talked with them after dinner about love. That discussion is the founding statement of the Christian community as a community of love. Now after they finish breakfast, Jesus talks with them about love again but in an even more intimate way. He asks Peter whether Peter loves him. At the Last Supper, Peter had sworn his undying love and loyalty, saying that he would lay down his life for Jesus. Jesus had answered with irony, nay, with resignation and pity, "Will you lay down your life for me? Very truly, I tell you, before the cock crows, you will have denied me three times." That is exactly what happened. Luke records that at the moment the cock crowed, Jesus who was being interrogated a short distance away turned and looked at Peter, and Peter wept bitterly.

Now imagine you were Peter. Jesus had treated you as leader of the disciples, and you had thought your love for him was so great that you would follow him to death. You had been brave enough to defend Jesus with a sword when he was arrested, but when the venue changed to the courthouse, you had denied that you even knew him. You were not under immediate threat, you were not being tortured, no one of importance was questioning you. But you denied three times all association with the one you had professed to love to death. And he had seen it. How would you feel when Jesus was killed before you could beg forgiveness? How would you feel in front of the other disciples who had heard Jesus' prediction of denial and had seen you do it?—the disciple whom Jesus loved was with Peter when he denied Jesus. I don't know about you, but I would be numb with grief. I would hate myself and doubt my capacity to love at all, or do anything worthwhile. When I'm numb with grief, I grade papers, the basic grunt work of a college professor. Peter went home to Galilee and said, "I am going fishing." Certain other disciples went along, also distraught and with nothing better to do. They spent a desolate black night on the boat, catching nothing. They were useless. Then in the morning Jesus came to them and told them how to haul in a bounty catch. And he fixed them breakfast. He would not accept Peter's denial nor the others' unhelpfulness and abandonment. He came back to them with food for life. And he repaired Peter's torn soul.

Do you love me, Jesus asked. Yes, Lord, you know I love you, replied Peter. Then take care of my people, said Jesus. So much for the first denial. Do you love me, Jesus asked again. Yes, Lord, you know I love you, said Peter. Then take care of my people, said Jesus. So much for the second denial. Do you love me, Jesus asked for a third time. "Lord, you know everything; you know that I love you," affirmed Peter, catching on to Jesus' gift of letting him reverse his denials three times. Now you will take care of my people, ordered Jesus, with the bands of love rewoven.

Although we ourselves rarely have dramatic circumstances like Peter's, how easy it is for us to deny Jesus. Most of us have opportunities to speak up for Jesus and his Way and we keep quiet or play down our own participation in that Way. Far more frequent and insidious, however, are the denials of his Way in our behavior. In our moments of religious wakefulness, we know about those denials and resent them. Like Peter and his friends, we might be a little ambivalent about meeting the risen Christ.

Yet the point of the Last Breakfast is that Jesus seeks out us deniers, feeds us for the journey, repairs our broken souls, and gives us the commission to take care of those whom Jesus loved, namely, everybody. The Last Breakfast is a culminating symbol of Jesus' Easter resurrection.

Contrast the Last Breakfast with the endings of the other Gospels. Mark's Gospel records no resurrection appearances at all. Luke's Gospel ends in Jerusalem with a final lecture to the disciples about the scriptures and a commission to proclaim repentance and forgiveness to all nations. Jesus then leads them out to Bethany whence he ascends into heaven. Matthew's Gospel ends with the disciples on a mountain in Galilee prostrating themselves before Jesus who tells them to make disciples of all nations and to teach them to obey. Instead of ascending to heaven, he says that he will be with them until the end of the age. The reference to "all nations" in Matthew and Luke is a change from Jesus' previous limitation of his mission to the children of Israel alone. There is, I sense, something a bit official and almost bureaucratic about these leave-takings in Matthew and Luke, obviously intended by the evangelists to lay out a mission for the church. The Last Breakfast, by contrast, is intimate in tone, with Jesus again serving his friends, enabling them to work again after their grief and confusion, repairing his particular friendship with Peter (and by analogy with us), and commissioning the disciples to carry on his Way. All three endings represent something authentic in the Christian tradition. Luke's emphasizes the preaching of repentance and forgiveness. Matthew's turns on the manufacturing model of making disciples. Both represent Jesus as something like a CEO addressing his employees. But John's commission is to feed the people with the bread of life. "Feed my sheep" is what a lover would say who has just fed breakfast to his friends.

The lesson to draw from this is that when we deny Jesus in our personal lives with laziness and narcissism, Jesus comes to us with spiritual nourishment and lets us tell him that we love him despite our denial. Then he gives us the job of taking breakfast to those others whose personal lives are in grief and confusion. When we deny Jesus in our social lives with cruelty and exclusion, Jesus comes to us with nourishing kindness and lets us tell him we love him despite our denial. Then he gives us the job of taking breakfast to others who are grief-stricken at their own cruelty or who are the victims of exclusion. When we deny Jesus by complicity in unjust social and economic structures, Jesus comes to us with food for restraint and social change and lets us tell him we love him despite our denial. Then he gives us the job of taking breakfast to others whose lives are threatened by injustice. When we deny Jesus with politics that make optional war on those who do not accept our economic, religious, and political values, arrogantly assuming that our military might is stronger than people's will for self-determination, cynically supposing that we can attack a people of God without their responding with a religious devotion to martyrdom, Jesus comes to us with a breakfast of humility and lets us tell him we love him despite what we've done to those people he's asked us to feed. Then he gives us the job of sacrificing our economy to the generation of our children's children to pay for peace and reconstruction.

Our future at this moment seems as confusing and unexpected as the future must have seemed to Jesus' small band of disciples gathered for the Last Breakfast. But they knew that nothing they could do by way of denial or flight could stop Jesus from offering them a breakfast of new life and a chance to restore their love. We know that too, for it has been the job of disciples through the ages to feed those whom Jesus loves down to our own time. The church at its best is the Last Breakfast of Christ. It is the meal at the beginning of the day. Now our job is to feed those who are in grief or confusion, who suffer cruelty or exclusion, are victims of injustice and war, including those who hate us and deny our good intentions. In our humility, may we be worthy of the Christ who appears among us feeding his flock. Amen.

15.

CALLING AND SENDING

Isaiah 6:1-8
1 Corinthians 15:1-11
Luke 5:1-11*

OUR TEXTS FROM Isaiah and Luke are two of the famous calling and sending passages in Scripture. One thinks also of the calling of Moses at the burning bush and the calling of Paul on the road to Damascus. In a vision, Isaiah was called into the divine throne room, so vast that the whole of Solomon's temple was the floor level, completely filled with the hem of God's robe. God was attended by flying seraphim and spoke directly to Isaiah himself. Isaiah saw God directly and was commissioned to deliver God's message to the people.

Luke's text tells of Jesus calling Peter, James, and John at the seaside to be his disciples and then to go out in the world as apostles of his Way. I don't know whether Peter and the others really were fishermen or whether the whole scene is an elaborate set-up for the wonderful line: "From now on you will be catching people," or as the King James version has it in Matthew: "I will make you fishers of men." The Gospel of John places the calling of Peter, James, and John in a suburb of Jerusalem and places the incident of Jesus telling them where to cast their nets for an overwhelming catch in a post-resurrection appearance. At any rate, when the disciples were called, they left everything and their lives were transformed with a mission, as was Isaiah's life.

These two texts have something special in common. Both Isaiah and Peter were totally thunderstruck at the divine glory, something Peter recognized only when he saw the miraculous catch of fish. The first response of both of them was to bewail their own sin. Isaiah said, "Woe is me! I am lost,

---

* Lections for the Fifth Sunday after the Epiphany, Year C.

for I am a man of unclean lips, and I live among a people of unclean lips; yet my eyes have seen the King, the LORD of Hosts!" Remember the biblical tradition that you cannot see God and live (Exod. 33:20). Peter fell at Jesus' knees and said, "Go away from me, Lord, for I am a sinful man!" John Calvin, the great reformer and theologian, began his *Institutes of the Christian Religion* with the observation that if you reflect on the glory of God, your attention immediately will be called to the fallen estate of human beings. And if you begin by considering the wretchedness of the human soul, your attention immediately will be drawn by contrast to the divine glory.

In the cases of Isaiah and the disciples, the divine encounter revealed to them not only God but also their own true identity as sinners. We don't know whether this was the first time they realized their sinful identity—I rather doubt it because they were all quick to identify themselves accurately before God. The point, however, is that confrontation with divinity immediately delivers the imperative to present yourself honestly before God. In doing so, you may find out who you really are if you don't know already.

The great twentieth-century theologian Paul Tillich said that everyone has an ultimate concern. The object of our ultimate concern ought to be God, of course, although most of us put other things first—our comfort, money, power, the needs of our ego. I think that Tillich was wrong in his claim that everyone has an actual ultimate concern, however misguided. Don't we all know people who aren't concerned about anything in an ultimate sense? Don't we have friends and acquaintances that flit from one concern to another, taking nothing very seriously? Don't we know people who are everlastingly "finding" themselves and, then not liking much what they find, abandon that identity and hunt for another? Doesn't the fact that we live in a consumerist society teach us subliminally to be concerned only about the next acquisition, which, as soon as we have acquired it, is not enough? We ourselves, of course, you and I, are indeed concerned to acquire deep meaning in life, but many of those other people are concerned only with the acquisition of the next thing. Surely you and I have ultimate concerns, but most of those others don't. We live in a society of proximate concerns. The passionate commitment to proximate concerns, to the acquisitions and little things, is a flight from the terrors of ultimate life.

The reason Paul Tillich believed, however naively, that everyone has an ultimate concern is that everyone, he said, is grounded by and in touch with the ultimate. Even when we don't know what the ultimate is and flit from one thing to another, the grounding presence of God in our lives drives us, he thought, to a passionate search for something about which it would be worth being ultimately concerned. He followed Saint Augustine in understanding the depths of each human soul to reach into the vastness of God; Augustine said that God is closer to us than we are to ourselves. Augustine said his soul was restless until it finds its rest in God because that is its natural place (see Augustine's *Confessions*). In fact, the restlessness of Augustine's soul was the divinity in the soul seeking its proper place. But Augustine himself from his youth was a driven man, earnestly seeking something to love ultimately. When he was young, he said, he was in love with love itself, with the idea of being a lover, and only as he tried out things to love, people and religions, did he mature. His conversion to Christianity was the choice of the right way of life, the Christian, through which he could acknowledge his soul's true home in God, and this was the fulfillment of his ultimate concern. Not many of us are like Augustine, with the passion of ultimacy driving us from our earliest days. Most of us don't take anything with ultimate seriousness. Or should I say, although you and I surely are ultimately serious, most of the others are not.

I agree with Tillich and Augustine that God lies deep in our souls. But we, or those others rather, are asleep to that divinity. People are under a deep anaesthesia to those frantic stirrings of ultimacy that drove the saints before they encountered God's call. Hence we need a shocking encounter with the ultimate to wake us up. We don't know much about Isaiah or Peter before their encounters with God and their special calls. They seem to have been successful, functional people. The events of their callings, however, brought them face to face with the ultimate, and they were changed people.

Alas, I doubt that we would be much impressed with the ultimate encounters Isaiah and Peter had. If a contemporary person were to experience Isaiah's vision of God in the throne room with the flying seraphim, the likely response would not be "Woe is me" but "Way cool—is this a video projection?" The same with Peter's inference from the huge catch of fish that Jesus was the Lord whom the unclean could not approach: we would treat it as a scientific question about how Jesus knew where the fish were. Neither Isaiah's vision nor Jesus' dramatic catch would give us "ontological shock," as Tillich called it, the shock of encountering something ultimate when we had thought only proximately important things were there.

If we have the ontological shock of encountering God, it might be in some sublimely beautiful thing, a sunset, a song, or a smile that reduces us to tears. More commonly we come up against ultimacy when suddenly faced with the ruination of our career, or the death of someone we love, or the imminent prospect of our own death. Or maybe we stumble on ultimacy not in external events but in a sudden recognition of our own abject failing, when the ultimate appears as a divine judge. Or maybe we find God as a creative power deep within our soul that we had not recognized before. But if we are asleep, we defend ourselves against the ontological shock of the ultimate in front of us. We do not attend carefully to what is beautiful. We deny or trivialize death. We lie to ourselves about our failings, always saying we can and will do better. And we tame the God within with the ropes of conventional expectations. I say, my friends, that we need to take down these defenses and wake up to ultimate reality. Creation abounds with opportunities for the divine encounter.

The price we pay for such an encounter, however, is the humbling admission of our own identity. No matter how good we are in comparative terms, in absolute terms we are bums. Please don't think that I am demeaning human virtues, of which you and I have many even if those others don't do so well. It's just that with us the virtues are so mixed with harms and vices that our identity is ambiguous, a mixture of good and bad. The encounter with the divine does not make us merely lament our sorry state. It makes us admit that state, to be honest. To test yourself for spiritual honesty, imagine yourself presented before God who sees and knows all things, face to face. To live before God is to live naked of any excuses and cover-ups. Encountering God strips us naked of all the shams by which we try to present a good face to the world or to ourselves. Even a sunset, observed with ultimate seriousness, does that.

Sometimes it seems to work the other way. Without any conscious encounter with God or anything ultimate, we interrogate ourselves about our personal identity and find nothing we like. We admit to ourselves our ambiguous morality, our self-deceptions, our flights from seriousness into a round of petty proximate concerns. We had been so proud of ourselves, so much in love with ourselves, that when we come to the shocking and unwelcome admission of moral vacuity we turn against ourselves with the condemnation and spiteful hate of a spurned lover. For a while we can take perverse pleasure in the ironic righteousness of our self-condemnation, but sooner or later that evaporates and we have just despair. No hope. Nothing. Nothing worthwhile is in the soul at all. Abandon hope all ye who enter honest into the soul.

But if you admit to absolute despair you will have found God. What is it that propels this internal examination but ultimate concern itself? Honesty that goes to the end finds the object of ultimate concern, the God whose creative power rushes through us like a mighty river. It's like John Calvin said: starting without God but with only the human soul, we immediately find God.

The result of the divine encounter and the turn to absolute honesty is a mission, a meaning for life. When Isaiah and Peter came to know who they were, they knew what they had to do. Of course they didn't know the details. God had to instruct Isaiah what to say, and Jesus had to shape the ministries of those who gave up their nets to follow him. Nevertheless, Isaiah and the disciples knew who they were relative to God, relative to the ultimate. Whatever confusions they later had, and the disciples had many, they lived through those confusions before God. They kept their proximate concerns in perspective and lived for those things that were of ultimate importance.

Let me tell you now that we all have been called. The simple gospel is enough for that. We have a mission to live before God as lovers, to create communities and human relationships that make love possible, and to pursue careers whose real meaning, whatever the job, is to extend Jesus' ministry of recreating the world in love. The exact content of your life and mine is dictated by the particular contexts in which each of us lives before God. We each must discern what our destiny of living in ultimate perspective is, and that depends greatly on the needs of the world around us. We are thrown into our particular situation and need to learn how to live ultimately in that world. The discernment of spirits, so as to detect the Holy Spirit, the Spirit that identifies precisely what is ultimate in our lives, is a gift devoutly to be prayed for.

Before that prayer for discernment, however, is my fervent prayer for you, that you encounter the God who shows you who you really are, who allows you to shuffle off your petty identity and take up an identity powered by ultimacy. You can fly to sublime beauty and God is there. You can suffer deep tragedy and God is there. You can sink to despair and God is there. You can encounter the wild creativity of our cosmos in the deepest recesses of your heart and God is there. I invite you to wake up to the divinity that is before and behind you, to your right and left, above and below, and deep within. When you come awake, you will know who you are. You will bear God's creative love in the shape and substance of your life. Without the resonance of ultimacy, your life is as a sounding brass or a clanging cymbal. With the ontological shock of the divine face-to-face comes honest life before God and an ultimate direction for life. Come, Holy Spirit, and reveal yourself, and us. Amen.

16.

WORKS THAT TESTIFY
(A COMMUNION SERMON)

Acts 9:36-43
Revelation 7:9-17
John 10:22-30*

RELIGION AND PSYCHOLOGY teach us that things often symbolize a lot more than they are by themselves. I remember the day in my freshman year when I learned about Sigmund Freud's theory of sexual symbolism. Suddenly my campus vanished and was replaced by a surreal landscape of towers and tunnels, fertile courtyards, and soaring arches bursting with light at the top. For all my new vision, however, I have to say that my love life was not improved. It really was just a bunch of college buildings. Similarly, some religious people like to see signs and portents in everything. Catching a cold is a sign of God's disfavor; finding a parking place in Boston during a Red Sox game testifies to the Parking Angel. Some people think that if they are wellborn, handsome, rich, or successful, surely God is with them and they deserve it. On the other side, many people take suffering as a sign that the victim deserves the suffering as punishment. In all those cases, things simply are what they are, for natural reasons, and the visions of cosmic meaning are mere projections, often pathological projections.

Nevertheless, there are occasions when the works people do, in fact, testify to something bigger and more important than the works themselves. Jesus, in our Gospel lesson, for instance, was being questioned about his real identity. Was he the Messiah or not? He did not answer by quoting scripture or giving a philosophical analysis of what messiahship

---

* Lections for the Fourth Sunday of Easter, Year C.

is as applied to himself. Rather he said, "The works that I do in my Father's name testify to me." People are what they do with what they have. Jesus was what he did, and his religious identity came from what he did in God's name. Of course Jesus' answer was more complex than met the eye. People in his time expected the Messiah to be a military leader like King David who would drive out the Romans and establish Jerusalem as the capital of the world where people from all nations would come to worship God. Jesus did nothing of the sort, although actions such as riding triumphantly into Jerusalem on Palm Sunday might have suggested that to some people. Rather, Jesus redefined what it means to be Messiah with his works, the humility of them, the humanity of them. Jesus claimed authority over his disciples by washing their feet. So Jesus' works not only testified to his identity as Messiah, they redefined the very role itself.

A more touching example in our texts of works that testify beyond themselves is the story in Acts of Dorcas, or Tabitha. I suppose that Peter's work of raising her from the dead is important because it testifies to the power of God that he exercised in the name of Jesus. But I want to call your attention to Tabitha's works rather than Peter's.

Notice that Dorcas was called a disciple. The term "disciple," or even "apostle," was not limited to the Twelve who had been especially named by Jesus. It applied to many people, including many women. The woman's Aramaic name, Tabitha, and Greek name, Dorcas, are both given; they mean "gazelle" in their respective languages. In the text they are alternated: Tabitha, Dorcas, Dorcas, Tabitha; obviously both are important. I suppose that this means that the Christian community in Joppa was a mixture of Aramaic-speaking Jews and Hellenized Jews who spoke Greek and that Dorcas was of the latter group. Or perhaps she was even Greek and not Jewish. If so, it was altogether more significant for Peter to visit her because he was slowly moving outside the definition of the Christian movement as wholly conforming to Jewish practice. This incident is related just before his experience with the Roman centurion Cornelius in which he came to declare all foods clean to eat, throwing over the kosher limitations. If Dorcas was in fact Greek, it was a bold move for Peter to minister to her.

What is most striking about Dorcas, or Tabitha, is that she seems to have been a longtime mainstay of the Joppa Christian community. This incident must have occurred within the first twenty years of the founding of the Christian movement. If we follow the chronology in the Acts of the Apostles, written by Luke as a second volume to his gospel, Tabitha's death and revival probably occurred much earlier than twenty years, say, within the first five or ten years. Yet Dorcas was settled with a group of widows, obviously a well-articulated group within the Christian community, and had worked with them for years making clothing. Most ancient Jewish and Hellenistic societies were organized around family life, and widows had little or no place unless they were supported by their children. The Christian communities from the very beginning gave a special place to the widows. What would our churches today do without the women who make the congregation the center of their lives, like a family?

Tabitha "was devoted to good works and acts of charity." When she sickened and died, the other widows washed her body and laid her out for what we would know as a wake and sent for Peter to come. The widows stood around fondling the garments she had made for them, the material results of her good works, the works themselves. Now to what did those works testify? They are not the works of a Messiah, or even of a great leader and now miracle worker like Peter. So far as we know, her good works were in paying attention to the needs of those around her. Like most of us, she attended to those in her community to whom she could relate directly, to the issues of security and health in her neighborhood, as exemplified in making clothing for people. Moreover, she must have done this superlatively, because her community so deeply mourned her that they sent for Peter and asked him to come without delay. Perhaps they hoped he could bring her back to life as Jesus had revived Lazarus but without the delay that had raised such tensions in the Lazarus incident. Whatever the hope, Dorcas was deeply loved for her charity and good works by those around who had come to know her as a person of charity and good works. Her works testified to the sanctity and healthy good life of the Christian community in Joppa. They testified to her responses to the needs of that community. They testified to the fact that the community could love her and fight against her death.

We, of course, need to do good works that testify to the grounds and obligations of our faith. Every one of us lives in a community with needs; what we do in response to those needs testifies to the quality of our faith. Let's keep the order right. It's not that we first have faith and then respond to the needs in proportion to our faith. It's that we first practice good works, and this determines the quality of our faith. Any of us can have right beliefs, but that does not mean we act upon them. Many of us go through existential trials to decide that Jesus Christ is our Lord and Savior; sometimes this decision costs great humiliation in front of secular friends. But even having made that decision, whether it's real depends on what we do. Let us present our deeds before a neutral observer, say, God, and ask whether, given what we do, it looks as if Jesus is our Lord and Savior. Our works testify to who we are. What testimony do we want them to give? What testimony do they in fact give? "By their fruits you shall know them."

I've been speaking of the testimony of our works as if we testify as individuals. But friends, we are in this together. A fundamental need in our community is for courtesy. We can each be courteous to one another, but we need to establish widespread social habits of courtesy. Poor people need help, and we individually can contribute to efficient charities, but we need collectively to develop an economy that minimizes poverty. To be marginalized is humiliating, and we can individually reach out to people who are marginalized because of race, class, sex, religion, or history. But we need collectively to develop a culture that embraces all without humiliation or deprivation of rights. We can individually express our political views when nothing much turns on it, but now that our country is occupying two countries that did not attack us, or even have the plausible means or will to do so, the needs for collective political responsibility are astonishingly compelling. Those of us who are Christians would like to say that our works, from common courtesy and local helping to responsible engagement of political affairs, testify to a Christian faith commanding love demonstrated by God in Christ, sustained by martyrs, carried down to us by the faithful, and made our responsibility by our baptism in these, our times.

So I invite you to the Communion table, the elementary work of Christian practice. From this table go out renewed in courtesy, charity, community building, and commitment to craft a society of which Jesus could be proud. Go out from this table comforted against the inevitable failure to be perfect in courtesy, charity, community, and politics, remembering that our kingdom is not of this world. Yet this table, showing Christ's presence here, manifests the fact that our kingdom, which is of God's world, is in this world. Here is where we have to be like Tabitha-Dorcas and live out our faith. Amen.

17

GOD IS NOT MOCKED (A SERMON PREACHED ON INDEPENDENCE DAY)

2 Kings 5:1-14
Galatians 6:7-16
Luke 10:1-12*

OR AMERICANS, THE Fourth of July is a quasi-religious holiday, something scholars call a function of our "civil religion." Civil religion is the set of practices that articulate the basic values of our national life that derive from religious sources. Thanksgiving is the other great American civil religious holiday, and it celebrates gratitude. Memorial Day is a lesser civil holiday celebrating military sacrifice, and Labor Day, also a lesser civil religious holiday, celebrating workers in democracy.

The Fourth of July celebrates freedom in two senses, first, independence from foreign domination and, second, self-determination of national life so as to foster individual freedom and to welcome of all kinds of people into citizenship. The Fourth of July is the most important of our civil religious holidays in that it rehearses those ideals in America's mythic self-understanding by virtue of which we think America is an exception to the usual course of nations. American exceptionalism is much justified in that this was the first modern democracy to be successful, the most pluralistic of cultures that still is united under the rule of law, the most vigorous and inventive economy in the world to have grown through a century of

---

* Lections for Proper 9, Sunday between July 3 and July 9, Year C.

turmoil, and the safest place for preachers such as myself to point out the religious improbity of the government without fear of retribution. To take Saint Paul's line that you reap what you sow, the successes of American exceptionalism reap the good seed sown by the revolutionary patriots.

My question for the day is, what is the Christian gospel, not the civil gospel, relative to the Fourth of July? The question is complicated by the fact that for many people, here and abroad, the United States currently plays a role more like the British in our revolution than like the colonists. It is our troops and mercenaries that occupy nations that did not attack us, our troops who are ambushed in out of the way places like Lexington and Concord, our troops who will be remembered for bombing wedding parties and killing women and children, our troops who are opposed by guerillas fighting for God and country. Like the British in the late eighteenth century, our motives for foreign wars seem to be a combination of righteous desire to advance proper democracy, as opposed to the French kind (if I may make a bad joke about the revolutionary conflict), and an imperial desire to establish a world economic order that works to the benefit of our economic elites.

Of course our current situation is much more complicated than this, and events can be read many ways. Nevertheless, like the British in the eighteenth century, our policies now seem to be driven by the thinking of empire, with both benevolent and malevolent motives. The benevolent motives have to do with imposing the grand values defining American exceptionalism on other peoples regardless of their own cultures of conflicting values. The malevolent ones have to do with reducing freedom to the freedom to pursue avarice. To much of the Muslim world, American freedom and democracy mean only those social forms that foster greed, with no transcendent moral principles whatsoever. However ignorant that view might be of the complexities of religious values in American history, it does point out that for a great many American colonists other than the founders in July 1776, economic promise was the most important motive for seeking independence from Britain and a representative government. The avarice sown in the American dream of independence is being reaped today in the enormous human and financial costs required to sustain empire. It seems that only the oligarchs are getting rich.

So what is the Christian gospel for Americans on this holiday? Luke tells of Jesus sending seventy of his disciples to all the towns he himself intended to visit. They were to be something like advance teams, of two people each, who would heal the sick and say that God was near and Jesus was coming, which might be the same thing. In the previous chapter Jesus had sent his intimate group of twelve disciples on a similar mission, promising them the power to heal and cast out demons. He did not promise the same power to the seventy, but they received and exercised it anyway. We Christians, like the seventy, are commissioned to go out into the world to heal, which means also peacemaking, and to proclaim that the kingdom of God is near, that is, that we live and are judged in the perspective of God. This is a crucial part of our gospel for today.

A strange part of Jesus' instructions to both groups of disciples was that they should go into a town and simply preach and heal. If someone accepts and hosts them, fine; if not, they should shake the dust of that town off their feet and go on to the next. Evangelistic success is not the point: presenting God's Word and power is the point. Behind this, however, is the fact that the villages included Samaritan and Canaanite communities as well as Jewish ones. Luke 9 tells of Jesus leaving a Samaritan community in a hurry because they objected to his orientation to Jerusalem—the Samaritans rejected worship at the Temple in Jerusalem in favor of worship on their mountain. The point is that Jesus sent his disciples to all the villages, not just the Jewish ones where they had a religious connection; this was in contrast to Jesus' earlier stance that he was sent only to the House of Israel. I take this to mean that in our own Christian mission of healing, including peacemaking, and preaching the presence of God, we should be true first to the message and mission, not to taking care of our own people first.

This is a hard lesson that we Christians should be in solidarity with Christians all over the world who heal and preach the presence of God before we are in solidarity with our national identity as Americans. Surely American Christians have great resources for healing and should deploy these all over the world, especially in poorer countries. Moreover, American Christians have an extraordinary peacemaking role in Iraq and Afghanistan. In no way does this mean that American Christians should interfere with the Iraqis' and Afghans' own efforts to establish a self-determining and efficient government—indeed peacemaking means getting out of their way and supporting their efforts as they see fit. Our prayers today should be long and fervent for the Iraqi government. As to preaching the proximity of the kingdom of God, I do not suggest that we or Christians anywhere try to convert Muslims to Christianity. Jesus had no conception of supporting one religion against others. He told the Samaritan woman at the well that the worship of God in spirit and in truth would transcend religious differences. Nevertheless Christians can testify to the critical presence of God by honoring the devotion of Muslims and by silently witnessing to the contradiction between God's peace on the one hand and the slaughter of innocents in terrorism and the beheading of kidnapped people for propaganda gain on the other. The most powerful Christian testimony for the Muslim world would be a direct criticism of the contradiction between Christian values and the brutality of empire.

This might be the hardest part of Jesus' commission to us, his disciples: to shake the dust off our feet when our own American towns and institutions reject the humility of healing and peace and the testimony that we stand in God's presence. How hard it must have been for the seventy abruptly to leave their own hometowns when they were not honored as prophets within it!

Jesus' instructions make the gospel particularly difficult for American Christians today. It is tempting in our purist moments to identify only with Christians around the world and forsake any special identification with America. Some of our more radical brothers and sisters do just this. Nevertheless, Christians who are Americans have special responsibilities for their democratic participation in American politics. We should insist that the Christian commitments to peace, justice, and kindness trump every other political motive in laws and policies where these are at stake. But political matters are devilishly complicated. Rarely are things as they seem. Ideological simplifications are the work of the devil. Political sound bites are Satan's syllables. Christians ought not abstract themselves from politics for the sake of a pure gospel; we should immerse ourselves in politics so as to think through the political ambiguities and complexities to how the gospel can be embodied.

Nothing in politics is of ultimate significance. Nothing political is a divine call. This is why civil religion is only a quasi-religion: sometimes it goes sour to give ultimate sanctions to nonultimate projects, which is demonic. To identify patriotism with religion is idolatry. Nevertheless, how we immerse ourselves in public life, including politics, is of very ultimate significance for our identity and service. It is how we present ourselves to God. Or as Jesus put it, God is coming so get ready.

Paul noted in the text from Galatians that God is not mocked. We mock God when we claim divine sanction for some political purpose. We mock God just as much when we withdraw from politics in the name of religious transcendence of conflict. Although Jesus announced that God's kingdom was at hand, he sent the disciples, and went himself, to witness to that. American Christians can celebrate the Fourth of July by committing our political lives to discerning what to do to embody peace, justice, and kindness as ways to love God with all our heart, mind, soul, and strength. I commend to you that political engagement that makes love of country a function of love of God.

As a final point, you all must have noticed that Jesus instructed his disciples to take no provisions, extra clothes, or money. They were to rely on the chance hospitality of the world to which they ministered. Jesus' point, I believe, was to warn the disciples not to think that making elaborate preparations would guarantee success. No matter how well we provision ourselves for ministry, the world will take what it will take and reject the rest. The surprise of the disciples was that, even though they had no expectations and were ready to move on if things did not go well, the demons fell before them. May we live in hope that peace, justice, and kindness are possible for our world. But let us also know that such worldly success is not the last word: Jesus' orientation to Jerusalem got him killed.

The ascetic approach to ministry that Jesus advocated sometimes might put us in the position of hungry beggars. Not everyone is lucky in hospitality. Nevertheless Jesus provided the disciples, and us, with a meal that is all sustaining. Here is the water of life and the cup of salvation. Here is the body of Christ that becomes our body. I invite you to join in the patriotic celebration of God's kingdom. I invite you to the table for the only provision that counts for the Christian journey. Come, let us give thanks and enter into the presence of Jesus. Amen.

DISCIPLESHIP

18

LAMENT OVER JERUSALEM (A LENTEN SERMON)

Genesis 15:1-12, 17-18
Philippians 3:17-4:1
Luke 13:31-35*

JESUS' LAMENT OVER Jerusalem is a puzzle. Why should he lament a city where he says he will be killed? To understand, we must put this in context. Our lesson describes an incident when Jesus had been teaching uncomfortable things. Immediately prior to our text is the parable of the householder who shut the door and would not admit his former guests who were evildoers. The householder is the Messiah, and those excluded "weep and gnash their teeth" to see the patriarchs and foreigners but not themselves admitted. Jesus repeats the familiar line, "Some who are last will be first, and some are first who will be last." Our text says that some Pharisees, who apparently were supporters of Jesus, warned Jesus to get out of the territory of Herod, fearing Herod's displeasure with such teachings. Though Jesus refused to be hurried, he said he would leave soon because it would not be appropriate for a prophet to be killed outside of Jerusalem. This was in reference to his own prediction, perhaps even intention, that he be killed in Jerusalem.

Now the Hebrew Bible mentions only one prophet being killed in Jerusalem. Second Chronicles said that Zechariah son of Barachiah was killed by order of the king; this was not the same Zechariah whose prophetic writings we have. The parallel passage in Matthew cites the murder of innocent people from Abel in Genesis to Zechariah in 2 Chronicles; in the order of the Hebrew Bible, Genesis is the first book and

---

* Lections for the Second Sunday in Lent, Year C.

2 Chronicles is the last, so the point is a generalized condemnation of murder from first to last. Jesus, I believe, was taking Jerusalem to be the symbolic center of Israel's betrayal of righteousness and of the covenant with God. Moreover, the betrayal was bloody murder, often directed against those who, like the Zechariah in question, were prophetic critics of the betrayal. Luke represents this as Jesus' self-understanding of his own role as prophet; remember that Luke's Gospel was written after everyone knew that Jesus was indeed killed in Jerusalem.

The lament over Jerusalem needs to be understood against the background of the covenant between God and Israel. Our Genesis text describes one of the covenant scenes between God and Abram, later called Abraham, in which the elderly, childless Abram is told he will have descendants as numerous as the stars in heaven. Abram believed God, and this belief was "reckoned as righteousness," a phrase Paul would later pick up to indicate the meaning of faith: for Paul, Abram was justified because of this faith in the promise against all the evidence (Abram and his wife were too old to have children). Abram sacrificed a heifer, a female goat, a ram, a turtledove, and a pigeon, split the larger animals in two, and walked between the halves carrying a smudge pot and a flaming torch to signify the covenant in which God, because of Abram's righteousness in believing the promise of heirs, would give his descendents the land from the Nile to the Euphrates. Many other dimensions to this covenant emerged later, and then the covenant that Moses recorded gave much more explicit definition to the nature of Israel's special relation to God. Finally God covenanted with David to keep his family on the throne so long as Israel was faithful to this rich, multisided covenantal relation that defined them as a nation of priests who, when they were holy, were allowed access to God's presence. This literally meant having representatives go into the temple's inner sanctuaries, and figuratively it meant living close to God in all things. Most of the prophetic literature of the Hebrew Bible has to do with complaints about Israel not living up to its end of the covenant, consorting with alien gods, and falling into terribly unjust practices, with God promising both punishments and mercy. When Jesus said that he had come to bring good news to the poor, proclaim release to the captives and recovery of sight to the blind, to let the oppressed go free, and to proclaim the year of the Lord's favor (Luke 4:18-19), he was presenting himself as the fulfillment of this prophetic tradition. And Jerusalem killed the prophets.

The theme of covenant, betrayal, and murder of the prophets is a sore point with Americans. The first European settlers in New England were explicit about founding a new society in covenant with God. The Puritan covenant was not about a place—any place would do. It was about a way of life of justice among peoples and about individual and corporate devotion to God. Of course greed was involved in the colonies as well, with devastating effects on the Native Americans, but the greed and the Indian Wars were known to be bad, to be failures of the covenant. The greatest failure of the American covenant was the inability to handle the problem of authority for its enforcement, an ancient biblical problem. By the time of the post-revolutionary constitutional debates, the notion of covenant had expanded beyond sectarian religion to embrace the Enlightenment themes of liberty, equality, opportunity, and self-determination for all, with a complicated government of checks and balances to foster protection of the weak and of minorities against the imposition of the will and culture of the majority. The American constitutional covenant embraced, in principle, people from any culture in the world who wanted to enter into the covenant of a pluralistic society with a willingness to make their way amidst a swarm of diverse ways of life. It welcomed the poor by offering opportunity. For over two hundred years, successive immigrant groups have made their way to America to develop American versions of their home cultures. In nearly every instance, the fabric of American cultures at the time had to be rent and re-sewn to make room for them, often with pain but nearly always successfully. The great failure, of course, was the case of Africans brought to America in slavery, a blatant contradiction of the constitutional principles at the time of its adoption and the source of a bloody civil war. Now, however, racism is recognized for the evil it is and is being amended on many fronts, however far we remain from a solution. The changes of immigration laws in the early 1970s allowed millions to come from Asian and Middle Eastern lands with cultures radically different from the European culture of the founders. No one can claim now that the United States is not in principle and often in practice a pluralistic nation based on a covenant to respect liberty, equality, opportunity, and self-determination.

As greed was the snake in the earliest American covenant, it has been a counter-theme in our national character ever since. It gathered explicit respectability during the presidency of Andrew Jackson when politicians touted the slogan that "to the victor belong the spoils." Greed was perhaps the greatest, though not only, component in the practice of slavery and racism, and it has fed America's adventures in imperialism in its wars with Mexico and Spain and then in the cultivation of a global economy that insists on free trade for others and protection for American interests. Greed is a legitimate interest in a democracy, however reprehensible it might be morally and debasing to the ideals behind the covenant. Yet greed never overwhelmed the higher ideals of the covenant. The American policies after World War II that rebuilt Germany and Japan and revitalized their regions of the world, that supported the United Nations to share power with all peoples, and that bound the world together with multilateral treaties about economies and the environment, were magnificent testimonies to a generous American spirit. They extended the ideals of the American covenant to a conception of an entire world of freedom, equality, and opportunity, with a right of national self-determination, however compromised the ideals were in many details.

In our own time, however, it requires a prophet to remember the generosity of the American covenant. Our government advocates a global economic system that paupers nations that cannot compete and destroys cultures that are noncompetitive. Our government responded to the criminal tragedies of 9/11, not with an international police action that would have been appropriate to counter an international terrorist organization, but with a bloated war on terrorism. In the name of that war, we have invaded and now occupy two countries that did not attack or threaten ours. Greed, not the covenant to respect liberty, equality, opportunity, and self-determination, seems to guide our foreign adventures. At home our government's tax policies favor the very rich while it withdraws social services from the poor that they need in order to have opportunity. On the one hand, our courts are now extending the rights of liberty, equality, opportunity, and self-determination to homosexual people, as they earlier had done to women and African-Americans, all of whom had been denied those rights. On the other hand, the government is threatening a constitutional amendment to enforce one culture's version of how those rights should be limited. Who will remind us of the covenant of liberty, equality, opportunity, and self-determination and of the generosity of Americans toward those of lesser freedom, unequal burdens, and frustrated opportunity? Like Jerusalem, America has not always been kind to its prophets. One need only remember the life and tragic death of Martin Luther King Jr. to recognize that fact.

Jesus did not lament over Jerusalem because it would kill him or because it had killed the prophets before him. He lamented because it had not been faithful to the covenant that made it a holy city. "How often have I desired to gather your children together as a hen gathers her brood under her wings, and you were not willing!" Our standing as American Christians is a complicated one. As Christians we should love all people, including those at enmity with America, and help first the least among our brothers and sisters. As Americans we have a natural desire to see America prosper in material goods, culture, and moral standing. Like Jesus, we cannot take up a condemnatory attitude toward our country, however much we might lament its current repudiation of its complicated founding covenant. Rather, our lamentation should be to take it under our wings as a hen gathers her brood. As Jesus went to Jerusalem to engage it, not repudiate it as Jerusalem had repudiated its covenant, we need to engage our country and its confusions now. Christians need to be their country's spiritual directors, its shrivers!

So let us pray for a spirit of honest analysis of America's policies abroad and at home, subjecting them to tests of righteousness, liberty, equality, opportunity, and self-determination. Let us pray for a spirit of courage to lift up and condemn the dross of bloated greed and power-madness. Let us pray for a spirit of power to speak these truths to those who hold power and can use it to silence prophets. Let us pray for a spirit of subtlety to understand the ambiguities of righteousness while upholding it and to communicate this at home, in the workplace, and on the street, to strangers and even to friends. Let us pray for a spirit of humility to see where our righteousness becomes false righteousness and our moral certainties turn out to be foolishness. Let us pray for a spirit of faith that shows Jesus' death to be the only saving one and that suffering on our part is not cosmically noble, only sad. Let us pray for a spirit of hope that sustains us when the enemy corrupting our covenant turns out to be our own interests and the institutions that sustain them. Let us pray for a spirit of love that keeps us engaged when we lose, that binds the love of our country to the love of all those other countries, and that never lets us think the voice of prophecy is ours against the villains because the voice of prophecy is God's and we all are the villains loved by God.

So come to the Communion table to join with other sinners grateful for God's prophetic blandishments. Come to the table to celebrate Jerusalem's murder that led to new life. Come partake of death's detritus that is yeast to cause righteousness to rise wherever Christians gather for the good grace of Christ. Though our covenants be broken, yet may they ever be renewed. Though we be blinded by greed, yet may our generosity be restored. Though Jerusalem's pride causes it to be toppled stone from stone, yet may it repent and be rebuilt. Gather at the table with those who lament our social betrayals and yet find seeds of resurrecting life everywhere. Gather with those whose love of country, neighbors, and self burns hot to purify our lives. Gather with those who pray to receive the holiness that brings us all to God. Behold God's covenant, God's betrayers, God's redeemer, God's saints, God's hospitality, our home. Everyone is welcome at this table, gathered under God's wings. Amen.

19.

THE CUP OF THE LORD (A PALM SUNDAY SERMON)

Luke 22:14-38*

PALM SUNDAY HAS an irony that can hardly be borne. Jesus entered Jerusalem like a king, riding a young donkey, which was supposed to symbolize a triumphant king in peacetime. His disciples formed a large courtly retinue. The people spread palm branches before him and shouted praise. By the following Friday he was dead, rejected by the people of Jerusalem—who chose the life of Barabbas, a murderer and insurrectionist, over his—and abandoned at least temporarily by even his own closest disciples. If ever there were a failed coup, this was it.

Let us not mistake the seriousness of this point. The people who welcomed Jesus into Jerusalem did indeed treat him like a legitimate king, a descendant of David, who would free Israel from the Romans and establish it as a sovereign kingdom under his own leadership. What Jesus himself really thought about that, we do not know, but he surely did let the people believe that. After finishing the ride into Jerusalem he went straight to the Temple, according to Luke's account, and drove out the people who made a profit on selling animals to be sacrificed, a kind of cleansing that asserted his own royal authority over the Temple. Whether this Temple incident really happened during his last week or at the beginning of his ministry, as the Gospel of John says, its effect was to convince the Roman governor and the chief priests, who had a delicate collaboration, that Jesus was challenging their authority. They expressed no fear of some vague spiritual authority in Jesus. If that were their worry, they would have

---

* Lection for Palm Sunday, Year C.

arrested his major disciples, too, so as to squelch his religious movement. The civil and priestly leaders were worried only about his rival political authority, which might be given him by the mob of people already upset by the Roman occupation.

The disciples, too, were expecting a royal victory for Jesus, according to Luke. Remember how they argued about which of them would have the highest status in Jesus' kingdom. Jesus told them they would be something like viceroys in his government, each judging one of the twelve tribes of Israel. Pitiful as it seems in contrast to the power of Rome, the disciples on the last night carried swords like a royal bodyguard and attempted to defend Jesus by force when he was arrested. Jesus had asked them to arm themselves before leaving the Passover supper, knowing that the authorities were looking for him.

All of this royal revolution business came to nothing. The Roman authorities stamped out the little threat Jesus posed by arresting and summarily executing him. His disciples abandoned resistance and went underground. Lest we think that the resurrection reversed Jesus' political fortunes, remember it did not. The resurrection appearances of Jesus to his disciples constituted brief stops on the way of his ascension into heaven, however you interpret that. Jesus left the field of earthly political combat, and the movement he started remained small and politically weak until it became the established religion of the empire under Constantine three centuries later.

Now perhaps Jesus himself did not intend a political kingdom. Perhaps his popularity as a teacher and healer was exploited by others who did want such a kingdom. According to the Gospel of John, Jesus told Pilate that his kingdom was not of this world and that if it were his disciples would still be fighting. In Luke's account, Jesus refused to admit to being the king of the Jews, saying only "You have said so." When Jesus was baited about paying taxes to Caesar, he took a coin, pointed out Caesar's image, and said to give to Caesar what is Caesar's and to God what is God's, effectively separating political from religious authority and ducking the issue. When his enemies tried to get him to say something seditious to the authority of either the Temple leaders or the Romans, he didn't. Of course the Gospel accounts we have of all this were written a full generation after the events, and the writers were trying to deal with the fact of the devastating end to any political aspirations Jesus' early movement might have had. We simply do not know what was in Jesus' own mind.

Nevertheless, the early Christians drew a clear moral from the events: the authority with which we should be most concerned is God's authority, not that of political power based on force of arms. When Christians do become engaged in political affairs and exercise political authority, as we should, the power to be sought should not be force of arms but the power of peacemaking. Within the New Testament itself, there is no clear ground for an absolutist pacifist position. I read the New Testament position to be that those with power have the responsibility to protect those without power from harm. This was an elementary meaning of the notion of the messiah from the Hebrew Bible. Having said this, we need to acknowledge Jesus' consistent preachments to overturn the ordinary worldly power relations. The first shall be last and the last first. The greatest, our text says, meaning the elders, should be like the youngest. The leader is the one who serves, and the Gospel of John illustrated this with the story of Jesus washing the feet of his disciples.

For us Christians today, reflecting on the triumphal entry into Jerusalem and the utter collapse of that project, several conclusions follow.

First, political dominance by force of arms is not a Christian project, however much that might seem tempting to those who have enough arms to overthrow their oppressors. Should they have enough arms to do that and more, we can be practically certain that they would quickly assume the role of oppressors themselves.

Second, Christian engagement in political affairs should be directed by an aggressive campaign of strategic pacifism. By "strategic pacifism" I mean the use of nonviolent techniques of the sort employed by Gandhi and Martin Luther King Jr., to raise consciousness, to embarrass oppressors, and to force the primary issue of hypocrisy, namely, oppression disguised as benevolence. The grace in the world is so rich and the depths of conscience are so powerful that strategic pacifism often works. If only the Jewish and Muslim traditions contained strong elements of aggressive nonviolence aimed at change for justice, the situation between Israel and Palestine in the Middle East would have been resolved long ago. They do not contain such traditions, however, and we have seen such pictures as Israelis in a helicopter gunship assassinating an old paraplegic in a wheelchair while leaving his prayers, not an innocent grandfather but the leader of Hamas who had sent children to their deaths as murderous suicide bombers. These in turn justify their actions with something like Nathan Hale's sentiment, his final words before being hanged by the British in 1776, "I only regret that I have but one life to lose to my country," outraged by the Israeli occupation of their land, which is deemed necessary to prevent the Palestinians from attacking Israel itself, which was planted by colonial forces that did not respect the thirteen hundred years of Muslim culture in the land, and so forth. Violence breeds violence and the cycle escalates. It boggles the mind that the United States has adopted the policy of enforcing an occupying power's political agenda by force in Afghanistan and Iraq after seeing the power of patriotic political insurgence in Palestine, not to speak of remembering the founding years of the United States.

Third, despite our best Christian efforts at peacemaking, when our own quest for power has become a mirror image of our opponents and the evil consists in the situation of violence itself, we still might have to engage in Christian battle to protect the weak. Reinhold Niebuhr was right that everyone loses in this situation, and the best alternative is the one that loses least in the moral scale. Public responsibility to the weak trumps personal virtue in a religion like Christianity that says the self is to be subordinated to the good of others. Glory be to God that Christianity is a religion designed for sinners.

Fourth, even the best strategy of peacemaking and reluctant warmaking has no divine guarantee of success. The lesson of Palm Sunday is that even the best political legitimacy, the loftiest ideals, the craftiest peacemaking, and the most strategic mix of persuasion and force can end up on the cross. Christianity does not count on success in the terms of this world's kingdoms. And we cannot abandon our responsibilities to this world or draw back from making ultimate sacrifices like Jesus. Despite our best efforts, we might fail to protect the weak and secure justice.

Fifth, the Christians' real success story has to do with binding our historical lives to God rather than winning on history's terms.

Moreover, the meaning of Palm Sunday is that we cannot relate ourselves to God without full engagement with the world. For Jesus, commitment to the world was a bitter cup. He did not want to drink the cup that God and history had given him. But had he snuck into Jerusalem rather than entering triumphantly, or snuck out of Gethsemane in the dark of night, it would have taught his disciples that the world does not matter. Jesus must have cried when he rode in triumph, knowing he would lose the world's game. But he bound himself to God in love and turned the losing of the world's game into truly winning the world. For, to become God's lover in the midst of history's confusions and alarms, its blind inertial forces and unbreakable cycles of violence and hatred, is to complete God's creation in our local place. To be God's lover means not giving up on the world, for God does not abandon the world. Jesus drank that cup, and so may we. When we are crucified, we each should still be able to say, "Father, into your hands I commend my spirit." Amen.

20

ARE YE ABLE?

Job 38:1-7
Hebrews 5:1-10
*Mark 10:35-45**

THE GOSPEL THIS morning contains the line made famous by the popular hymn, "Are Ye Able," written at Boston University in 1926 by Earl Marlatt who subsequently became dean of the School of Theology. Marlatt's verse begins, "'Are ye able' said the Master, 'to be crucified with me?' 'Yea,' the sturdy dreamers answered, 'to the death we follow thee.' Lord, we are able. Our spirits are thine. Remold them, make us, like thee, divine. Thy guiding radiance above us shall be a beacon to God, to love, and loyalty." Marlatt's hymn is straightforward Wesleyan theology, which does not always agree with the Reformation emphasis on divine initiative alone. Wesley held that although God's grace saves us, we have to receive it, and in receiving it we have the responsibility for sanctification. For Wesley, if not for Luther and Calvin, salvation has to transform actual character. Marlatt sang "Our spirits are thine. Remold them, make us, like thee, divine." That's a clarion plea for holiness that centers our faith through times of trouble.

Mark's Gospel is subtler than Marlatt's hymn, which indicates the complexity of the passage only by calling Jesus' interlocutors "sturdy dreamers." In the Gospel story, James and John, who are identified as the sons of Zebedee, came to Jesus in private with an adolescent request. In Matthew's account of the story, it was not James and John themselves, but their mother, who made the request. I would guess from this that they were very young disciples, perhaps college age, perhaps a freshman and sophomore respectively, identified by their father's name and spoken for

---

* Lections for Proper 24, Sunday between October 16 and October 22, Year B.

by their mother. In Mark's account the boys first asked Jesus to promise to do for them whatever they asked. Jesus sidestepped that and asked what they wanted. They answered that they wanted to sit on his right hand and left when he reigned in glory. How presumptious! Perhaps both were sophomores. They surely were dreamers!

In a sermon on Jesus as friend, Professor Wesley Wildman has pointed out how gently Jesus responded to them, not ridiculing their dreams nor rebuking them with a lecture about servant ministry as he later did the other, presumably older, disciples when they had a jealous fit about James and John. Rather, Jesus gently told them they did not know what they were asking. He asked whether they were able to drink the cup he would drink and be baptized with his baptism. By the "cup" he meant his destiny to be crucified; later in the Garden of Gethsemane he prayed that this cup would pass from him but affirmed the courage to drink it if it were his true destiny. By his baptism he meant following his Way, what would later be called the Christian Way, which was subject to much persecution. Mark's Gospel was written about forty years after the crucifixion in the midst of Roman persecution, and his readers would know what those expressions meant but the boys did not have a clue. As sturdy dreamers, they answered, "We are able!" Jesus must have sighed at the innocence of these young disciples he loved. He told them only that it was not his right to grant who was to sit at his right hand and left.

Mark pictures Jesus as a lonely man, surrounded by enthusiastic followers who do not understand the horror to come or why that has to be borne. Peter had proclaimed him the Messiah and then rebuked Jesus for gloomy talk about persecution, death, and resurrection; Jesus responded, "Get behind me, Satan." Young James and John had no better understanding.

The fate of the disciples, in fact, was to drink Jesus' cup of suffering and to be baptized with his Way that brought persecution. According to Acts, James was killed by Herod Agrippa in a great persecution of the church. Tradition has it that John, who was identified as the Beloved Disciple, escaped with his life to live to a very old age on the island of Patmos, writing his Gospel and the Letters bearing his name. However romantic and innocent their sturdy dream that they were able to follow Jesus, in point of fact they were able. And through the vicissitudes and persecutions of the church they, like Jesus, were made perfect through suffering, to use the phrase from the Letter to the Hebrews.

For us, the situation seems to be dangerously similar. Christians don't have Romans out to persecute them these days, although Christians in many parts of the world do practice their faith in jeopardy of their lives. The specific danger I have in mind, however, is moral conflict that has the power to distort, pervert, and ultimately ruin Christian faith and practice. By moral conflict I mean issues on which good Christians take opposite sides, issues so identified with the heart of their faith that the intense passion of loving God with all their heart, mind, soul, and strength and their neighbors as themselves—that passion gets transferred to their moral stand. Transferring infinite religious passion to moral stands is dangerous. Consider three examples, out of the dozens that could be called to mind.

Abortion is a moral conflict so old to Americans that it has been reduced to slogans, pro life versus pro choice. How could such a complicated issue be reduced to slogans? It raises questions about the role of law in regulating medicine, about the morals of medical practice, about communal responsibility for the care for families and for people born without families, about the institutions and various conditions of marriage, as well as the obvious questions of freedom and self-determination, the definition of human life, the claims of human life on legal and social protections, and the responsibility of religion to think through such complex issues and to protect the weak.

The important thing to notice is that the issue is one of balancing competing values. Even the slogans, pro life and pro choice, show that the moral conflict is over how to balance values that nearly all people share. Who could be against protecting prenatal children? Who could be against women's rights to determine how their bodies are to be used? Yet instead of approaching the abortion debate with humility, fear, and trembling at its complexity, often Christians leap to choose crude sides with demonic passion.

The second example is homosexuality, conflict over which has reached the Supreme Court of the United States. Moral conflicts in politics have centered on antidiscrimination protections and legal rights of homosexual partners likened to marriage. Religious denominations, especially the Protestant Christian ones, nearly all are in desperate conflict over a number of issues concerning homosexuality. The most recent is the response of Episcopalians to their denomination's election and confirmation of a gay bishop in New Hampshire. Again, the moral conflict is a matter of balancing values that are nearly universally held. Who can be against the right of gay and lesbian people to fulfillment and happiness? Who can be against social responsibility for the moral structures of such institutions as marriage and ministry? Passions in the moral conflicts about homosexuality are so high that surely more than sexual ethics is involved. It seems a matter of religious identity.

The third example is the series of moral conflicts that have arisen in connection with the recent wars in Afghanistan and Iraq. While seemingly topical issues raised by events such as 9/11, the conflicts have raised to consciousness deep divisions about fundamental political values. What are the conditions that should be met to justify the United States becoming an aggressor nation as it has? Have they been met? Patriots on one side justify the use of overwhelming force by the righteousness of the cause. Patriots on the other side condemn the use of force because the cause is not righteous. These conflicts have not even begun to be articulated with the subtlety and complexity they obviously need. And yet Christians in good faith are divided against each other with holy passion.

Are we able to follow the Christian Way while we are persecuted by our own divisions on these and the many similar issues that divide Christians?

Two tempting strategies exist that I believe will lead to disaster. One is to treat religion as a private matter and refuse to address in church public issues such as abortion, homosexuality, and war and peace. In practice, this is what many Protestant pastors attempt to do, for the obvious reason of maintaining harmony within the community. The ongoing life of religious communities has many more values than just the resolution of these hot-button issues, and the cost of addressing them within the community is very high. Nevertheless, religion is not merely private, and when it deliberately blinkers itself against the issues about which people feel so passionately it makes itself irrelevant to the real religious issues.

The other disastrous but tempting strategy is for the church to address issues like these without a solid theological base, as if they were merely political or moral issues. Without its theology, Christianity has nothing in particular to offer to the resolution of deep moral conflicts. Many preachers, however, get so excited about taking a "prophetic" stand on moral issues that the self-righteous fact of their convictions pretends to excuse them from justifying the convictions. Yet surely, the convictions need to be justified with careful argument, with sensitivity to the ways people with conflicting convictions weigh values, and with humility based on the plain recognition that our judgments are fallible at best. Only careful theology can put the measuredness of moral analysis and judgment in ultimate perspective. The justifications need to be theological to address the reasons for putting infinite religious passions on moral convictions.

However much pastors would like to avoid conflict, the riveting moral conflicts of our time need to be brought into the church so that we can live them through with intelligence and love. No pulpit can escape the obligation to articulate, analyze, and offer guidance, with all humility, on the issues that shape the preacher's watch.

I invite you into the arduous task of sustaining a congregation in the midst of deliberately addressed conflict. Those who agree with the analyses and judgments articulated from the pulpit should do so with arguments at least as complex as the preacher's and should share with those around them their better ones. Those who disagree should take that fact as a special sign that they belong in the congregation to correct the preacher and those whom he or she might mislead. To stay away in anger or because of the pain of conflict would be to fail the community. I invite you into a theological conversation that will not run from divisive issues but will incorporate the process of dealing with divisions in pursuit of truth into the life of the community. The church should be a place you can come home to in order to address the religiously weighted conflicts of our time, not a place that suggests you escape. As Jesus said, the Way leads to crucifixion, and to many in the Church these moral conflicts feel like that. Beyond the crucifixion, however, is the new life of resurrection. Like love in a family, love in the Christian community can bear up through the realities of conflict. Because the church is Christ's family, resurrection love calls us to the joy of being real when faced with conflict, staying in love with those with whom we struggle. A Christian community that embraces and works through conflict with brothers and sisters shines with the redeeming light of the Father, Son, and Holy Spirit. Are we able to sustain the Christian Way when it engages the flesh and blood issues that command conflicting religious passions? I invite you to answer, "We are able!" Amen.

21

READING SCRIPTURE IN CONFLICTS (A REFORMATION SUNDAY SERMON)

Job 42:1-6, 10-17
Hebrews 7:23-28
Mark 10:46-52*

ONTEMPORARY LIFE CONFRONTS us with divisive moral conflicts that have serious religious dimensions, including such issues as abortion, homosexuality, and war. Christians of good faith are in deep conflict with one another about these and other issues, and I would argue that the conflicts should be addressed within the church. Christians need to hold their divisive passions in check and work through the issues together. Those of us who occupy the pulpit have a special obligation to provide analysis and guidance around these issues.

Today I want to consider the role of Scripture in such deep moral conflicts because Scripture is the first authority for Christian discussion. Although in a reflective sense the Bible bears upon all moral conflicts in ways mediated by traditions of analysis, the Bible does not directly address abortion or the war in Iraq. So I will discuss the biblical background of homosexuality as our test case.

---

* Lections for Proper 25, Sunday between October 23 and October 29, Year B. Other suggested texts are Genesis 18–19; Leviticus 20:8-18; Matthew 10:5-15; Romans 1:18–2:1; 1 Corinthians 6:9-11; 11:2-16; 1 Timothy 1:8-11.

The story of Sodom and Gomorrah was long taken to be the definitive condemnation of homosexuality. (The Bible speaks only of homosexual acts, never of homosexuality as a lifestyle or orientation.) The Sodom text is Genesis 19. You will remember that Abraham's nephew, Lot, was visited in Sodom by two angels who looked like men. All the men of the town, young and old, gathered outside Lot's house and demanded that the angels be sent out to them to be raped. Lot offered his two virgin daughters instead. When the townsmen started to break down the door the angels struck them blind and led Lot and his family out of town while God destroyed Sodom and Gomorrah with fire and brimstone. In time, the name sodomy became synonymous with homosexual and some disapproved heterosexual acts, but that time, surprisingly, was not until the European Middle Ages, about the tenth century. I commend to you a book by the scholar Mark D. Jordan called *The Invention of Sodomy in Christian Theology*, published by the University of Chicago Press in 1997, for a documentary history of how the story of Sodom and Gomorrah came to be associated with homosexuality. In biblical times and long afterward it was associated instead with a brutal violation of hospitality. Raping a person under the hospitality protection of a town member was about as bad as inhospitality could get. A parallel to the Sodom story, similar in language and plot, is in Judges 19, according to which a visitor to Gibeah was taken in by a townsman, the men of the town demanded he be sent out to be raped, his concubine was sent out instead, and she was raped to death, leading to a disastrous war. In those days, hospitality was valued so high, and women's lives so low, that protecting one's guest, even when a stranger, was worth sacrificing women you love. Westerners do not share that balance of values now. That the story of Sodom and Gomorrah was taken in biblical times to be about violations of hospitality is confirmed by Matthew 10:5-15, in which Jesus says it will be worse in the last judgment for the towns that are inhospitable to his disciples than for Sodom and Gomorrah.

Let me remark here on an important point for biblical understanding. The authors of the biblical books shared with their intended readers a particular imaginative background or context in which what they wrote made sense. This imaginative background contained cultural assumptions, such as the high premium put on hospitality, the low premium put on women, and the acceptability of slavery. It also contained scientific assumptions, such as that if you go up far enough you get to heaven and that there is a world of angels and spirits to which we have access. Most of us in the

West now have a vastly different imaginative background from that of biblical times, especially regarding matters such as physical cosmology, the spirit world, slavery, the role of women, and even hospitality. Many contemporary Christians in Africa engage the world with an imaginative background rather like that of biblical times, sharing assumptions about spirits and women, for instance. For them there is little cognitive and emotional dissonance over such matters. Most of us Westerners, however, feel sharp cognitive and emotional dissonance with much of the ancient imaginative background. We always have to distinguish the religiously binding truth in Scriptures from the cultural and scientific assumptions in the ancient imagination that we reject, for good reasons. We need to work around elements in that imagination to which we believe our own moral and intellectual world is superior, say, about slavery as an evil, the equality of women, and scientific cosmology. We can dismiss the biblical readiness to sacrifice women in order to protect the honor of hospitality as deriving from a cultural assumption that we reject. The contemporary Islamic societies that sacrifice women for honor strike us with horror. How shall we read what the Bible says condemning homosexuality? Does it come from mere cultural assumptions that we rightly reject? Or is it religiously authoritative?

The book of Leviticus is clear in condemning homosexual acts. Chapter 20 repeats and expands upon a list in chapter 18, saying you should not lie with a male as with a woman in a long agenda of proscribed acts having to do with adultery, incest, bestiality, child sacrifice, sex during menstruation, witchcraft, and cursing one's father or mother. Scholars know this list as the "Holiness Code." Death is the punishment for adultery, child sacrifice, cursing father or mother, incest with mother-in-law or daughter-in-law, bestiality, and lying with a man as with a woman. Banishment or barrenness is the punishment for the other forms of incest, sleeping with a menstruating woman, and using mediums or wizards. All the laws are directed only at men even when women are involved in the proscribed behavior and are punished. Women were not regarded as sufficiently important moral agents to be addressed in law.

Does anyone today accept the Holiness Code fully and literally? Few of us would put to death people for the acts Leviticus proscribes. There are violent gay-bashers who kill people and do follow the biblical commandment to put to death men who lie with men as with women; nevertheless, such gay bashers are regarded in the United States as murderers. That we reject or seriously modify the biblical approach to punishment means we do not follow a purely biblical rule for morals and that we already make discerning judgments about what to accept. We in the West do not believe in witches and would be very slow to believe that cursing parents deserves the death penalty. Concerning the proscription of lying with a man as with a woman, should we liken that to child sacrifice, which we condemn, or making love during menstruation, which we do not condemn?

Turning to the New Testament, no mention of homosexuality or homosexual acts is ascribed to Jesus, although he repeatedly condemns adultery, divorce, greed, and other sins. No author in the New Testament except Paul mentions homosexuality, unless the author of 1 Timothy is someone other than Paul, which probably is the case. In 1 Corinthians, Paul clearly lists homosexuals in what scholars call a "vice list" along with fornicators, idolaters, adulterers, thieves, the greedy, drunkards, revilers, and robbers. In 1 Timothy, the list includes the lawless, disobedient, godless, sinful, unholy, profane, those who kill parents, murderers, fornicators, slave traders, liars, and perjurers. The word used in both 1 Corinthians and 1 Timothy for homosexuals is *arsenokoitai*, which is a rough Greek translation of "lying with a man as with a woman." First Corinthians uses an additional word, *malokoi*, which means "soft" and probably referred to the passive, perhaps younger partner. Paul has other vice lists that do not include any reference to homosexual acts or desire (Gal. 5:19-21; 1 Cor. 5:10-11; Rom. 13:13).

In Romans 1, which is the only biblical mention of homosexuality as more than an item in a list, Paul says that all nations know that God is Creator but that people suppress this knowledge with idolatry, become confused by sin, and "exchange natural intercourse for unnatural," women with women and men with men. This is the only mention of female homosexuality in the Bible. Scholars have debated what "natural" and "unnatural" meant in Paul's world, based on Greek philosophy. Part of what is meant is the hierarchical ordering of things Paul describes in 1 Corinthians 11. God is the head of Christ, "Christ is the head of every man, and the husband is the head of his wife" (11:3). A man is the image and reflection of God, and woman is the reflection of man. "Indeed, man was not made from woman, but woman from man. Neither was man created for the sake of woman, but woman for the sake of man" (11:7-9). In Paul's culture, although not all Hellenistic cultures, sexual relations reflected those hierarchical relations between the sexes. Sexuality was conceived always to have dominant and submissive partners. It was natural for a man to dominate a woman but unnatural to dominate a man who was supposed to be his equal. A sexually passive man is unnatural because men are supposed to dominate in sex. Similarly with women, the active sexual partner is unnatural because women are supposed to be sexually dominated. It is not the case today, I should note, that homosexual, or even heterosexual, relations always have dominant and submissive partners.

In many parts of the world the hierarchical dominance of men over women, in sex as in other matters, is enthusiastically asserted, often on these or other biblical grounds. Some traditional Asian, African, and Islamic societies are close to this biblical tradition. For most Americans, however, that dominance relation has been successfully challenged by an ethics of equality and reciprocity that largely has been written into law. Although feminists might claim that true equality is yet to be achieved, our current American customs and law are very far from the oppressive biblical model. Most liberal, moderate, and even conservative Christians reject the extreme cultural model of male dominance and female subservience expressed in Paul's writings. Even Paul qualifies his own hierarchy by saying, in our 1 Corinthians text that men and women are mutually dependent and that really both come from God. He says in Galatians 3 that gender differences like ethnic and slavery differences make no difference for those in Christ. The Gospels are filled with stories of Jesus treating women as equal to men in deserving respect and attention. The dominance hierarchical model is in strong conflict with the model of reciprocal love already present in the Bible, which applies to sexual love as well as friendship and social roles. To the extent that Paul regarded homosexual acts as unnatural because they perverted the so-called "natural" hierarchical dominance relations between men and women, that sense of unnaturalness is to be set in opposition to the biblical ideal of being one in Christ and friends among whom true leadership or dominance is a matter of service. Whereas hierarchical dominance might be natural in the sense of being the customary way, that cultural assumption was criticized and rejected, however unevenly, by the biblical ideal of the unified community of God's children.

The few biblical references to homosexuality need to be understood as part of a larger cultural imagination defining the relative roles of men and women in a dominant relation that includes sex as well as other matters. Our contemporary Christian brothers and sisters (Islamic as well) who share some of those assumptions of male dominance are likely to share the Levitical and Pauline condemnation of homosexuality as unnatural to the hierarchy. I count myself among those who reject that part of the imaginative background of the ancient world and find it troubling in contemporary society anywhere in the world. The women's movement has introduced a reformation to the Christian church far more profound than the Protestant Reformation that we also commemorate today. The women's movement is global, and all religious cultures are feeling its effects. It is the only element of moral progress in civilization that matches the scientific progress of the last several centuries.

Not everyone agrees, of course, with the ideals of equality and reciprocity among men and women, and the argument in that respect must take into account many considerations other than biblical ones. With regard to the Bible, however, I believe that the liberating gospel itself is so central to the great drama of creation and redemption that it thoroughly trumps the cultural assumptions of hierarchy. With that, the Levitical and Pauline condemnation of homosexuality as unnatural, because it confuses the hierarchy, falls to the ground. The explicit condemnations of homosexual acts in the Bible stem from a hierarchical culture that denigrates women and forces all people into relations of dominance and passivity. That culture is incompatible with the larger themes of the Christian gospel. Therefore I see the explicit biblical condemnations of homosexuality as merely reflective of a culture against which the church should witness, and as nonbinding in any authoritative way on our current moral reflections, unless extra-biblical considerations prove the contrary.

Let me close by reminding us of the larger scale of the Christian gospel, the grand story of creation and redemption. Created with the infinite bounties of God's grace, we are rich beyond measure and yet have let ourselves be estranged from God. This estrangement affects everything we are and do, including our sexuality. Our redemption in Christ, for which God be praised, allows us to overcome estrangement and, in sanctification, redeems our lives in all aspects that can be corrupted. Is homosexuality nothing but the corruption of heterosexuality, as Leviticus and Paul can be read to say, and therefore to be given up as part of redemption? Or is it a form of sexuality with integrity of its own, subject to alienation but also capable of being redeemed, and therefore to be lived out in a holy way by those whose impulses are for same-sex love? The scriptural case for the former is ruined by its connection with the corrupted hierarchical dominance model of human relations. The scriptural case for the latter celebrates the goodness of creation and the sanctifying grace of redemption.

Redemption also means, however, engaging with love and respect those Christians who share the ancient world's assumptions about hierarchical dominance and persuading them that those assumptions are counter to the central trajectory of the gospel. If my conviction is mistaken, it is the obligation of those who oppose it to engage those of us who hold it and persuade us lovingly of the error. That would be the way to engage moral conflict within the Body of Christ. Amen.

22.

NATURE, CULTURE, RIGHT, AND HOLINESS

Isaiah 25:6-9
Revelation 21:1-6a
John 11:32-44*

IN THIS SECTION I have been dealing with how the church should
handle passionate and divisive conflicts among Christians about moral
issues such as abortion, homosexuality, and war. Other religious communities also struggle with such conflicts. The previous sermon talks
about the appeal to Scripture in the conflict over homosexuality and
argues that the very few mentions of homosexual acts in the Bible reflect
cultural assumptions about dominance and subservience between men
and women that themselves are wrong and that should be corrected by
the Christian gospel. Here I want to consider other arguments about
homosexuality that do not have to do particularly with biblical references.

Homosexuality is usually claimed to be unnatural by those who oppose
it, and this claim is often a very deeply held emotional conviction, a gut
feeling. Most hold this conviction because they have been taught it. When
we ask whether it is justified, however, the first question has to be what is
meant by "unnatural"? Perhaps one or more of several things, and the
church needs to sort them out. The biblical discussion before this considered the case that social custom dictates that all sexual relations should be
of dominant over submissive partners and that men should be dominant
and women submissive. In this case male homosexuality is "unnatural"
because one partner needs to assume a submissive role, and female homosexuality would require one to assume a dominant role. If, to the contrary,

---

*Lections for the first Sunday in November, Year B.

the social custom emphasizes equality and reciprocity instead of a hierarchy of dominance, homosexual relations would not be unnatural in this sense. In many parts of the Western world, we have, in fact, substituted suppositions of equality and reciprocity for the ancient world's hierarchical assumptions and often have written them into law.

But same-sex desire might be unnatural in a deeper biological sense. Many in the ancient world believed that each thing has its own purpose or final cause, as Aristotle put it (though not everyone expressed the view as carefully as Aristotle). The sole purpose of sex, according to many of the ancients and some of our contemporaries, is procreation. They say that any use of sex for purposes other than procreation is unnatural because it is contrary to its purpose. Following this line, many Christians have condemned contraception and solitary sex, as well as gay and lesbian sex. Aristotle and the other philosophers who believed procreation is the purpose of sex saw it in the larger picture of the continuity of the species.

Contemporary biologists agree, of course, that sexual behavior is necessary for the continuity of the species but with a significant shift from ancient thinking. We now understand sex and continuity in terms of populations, not individuals. A given group or population needs sufficient new births to fill its ecological and social niche. When the niche expands or a disaster decimates the population, more children are needed, and in hard times the birth rate needs to go down. Within a population, however, not everyone, or every couple, needs to have children, so long as the group as a whole produces enough children for its niche. So whereas the ancient world put a terrible onus on barren women, we do not, so long as the population has enough fertile women for an appropriate birth rate. Moreover, not every sexual act of a couple that wants children and can have them needs to be potentially fertile, only enough so as to have their children. Hence contraception might well be used to time the birth of children by a couple that wants to have many. It is not biologically unnatural for some people never to marry or have procreative sex. By the same token it is not unnatural in the modern biological sense for some people to be homosexual and to have sex that is never procreative so long as others in the population reproduce so as to fill the niche. Nonreproductive sexual impulses, including same-sex ones, have a biologically natural place in a larger reproductive population. Christians who believe homosexuality is contrary to biological nature need to come to terms with the modern definition of nature in population biology.

If not biologically unnatural, homosexuality might be culturally unnatural, as so many people argue, perhaps not distinguishing this from biological nature. Societies organize themselves into families, and families are intergenerational. The natural cultural expectation is that one's children will have children. Some of the deepest opponents of homosexuality I know argue from bitterness about the fact their children will not give them grandchildren. To fit into organized society by living out an intergenerational family seems natural. That's how ordinary life defines itself for most people. The pull of intergenerational social roles is so great that many gay and lesbian couples want to serve as parents and do so by adoption, artificial insemination, or temporary heterosexual liaisons, perhaps even marriages. Gay and lesbian couples sometimes become parents in part to satisfy their own parents' longing for grandchildren.

That intergenerational family life is a culturally natural way to live does not mean, however, that it is the only culturally natural way to live. I know of no society in which everyone gets married to have children. When Jesus defined marriage as a man leaving his family to become one flesh with his wife there was no mention of children. Most societies have celibate social roles and also roles for sexual life without or apart from marriage. Many heterosexual couples marry who do not have children, for one reason or another, and there are natural places in our society for couples like that. Why are there not natural places in our society for gay and lesbian people to live together as couples or in other social arrangements? There is no reason, so long as those social places do not inhibit the general welfare and richness of society. Why should we not enrich social diversity with social roles that fulfill the happiness of gay and lesbian people?

The moral weight of some social roles, such as marriage, is more complex than I have indicated so far here, and in the next sermon I talk about the normative ritual character of social roles in connection with marriage.

Some people object to homosexual life, or lifestyles, on moral grounds. They complain about pornography, violent abuse, pedophilia, shallow promiscuity, or sex acts that seem gross to them. Surely many issues of sexual behavior have important moral dimensions, but they apply equally to heterosexual and homosexual behavior. Like heterosexual behavior, homosexual behavior can be immoral, degraded, and in deep need of amendment and redemption, not because of its sexual orientation but because of how that orientation is lived out. As to sex acts that seem gross to some people, they do not seem gross to those who find fulfillment in them.

In sum, whereas I argued in the sermon before that the Bible does not warrant believing homosexuality to be intrinsically sinful or immoral, I've argued now that is it not sinful or immoral because it is biologically unnatural or because societies ought to regard it as culturally unnatural. Gay and lesbian people might be thieves and murderers, disrespectful to parents and abusive of partners, lazy, gluttonous, drunkards, prideful, deceitful, and ready to use sex for demeaning and selfish purposes, just like heterosexual people. From these vices, they and everyone else need redemption. But gay and lesbian people should feel no guilt at all for their same-sex desire as such, I believe. They are no less creatures of God in their sexuality than those with other-sex desire, and both together can contribute to the flourishing of the human community.

The Christian church, like most other religions, has inculcated guilt and self-hate into gay and lesbian people, and that has been a grievous mistake. As the church should apologize for its complicity to those who have been enslaved because the Bible endorses slavery and to women because the Bible endorses their humiliating subordination to men, so it should apologize to gay and lesbian people whom it has demeaned on mistaken biblical and philosophic grounds. Thank God, through such contrition the church still can carry on God's work of redemption.

Now I'm sorry that the clarity of this conclusion cannot stand by itself. Giving recognition, respect, freedom, power, and support to gay and lesbian people is not the only value to which we must attend, however important and overdue it is. Many competing values also exist—for instance, harmony in families, the church, and society—that are threatened by a challenge to the cultural assumption that homosexuality is sinful. The values having to do with social harmony are extremely complicated. So long as many people believe that homosexuality is sinful, and do so out of deep convictions lodged in the assumptions through which they see the world, any challenge to that stigmatization of gays and lesbians threatens family, church, and social order. For all their insistence that their lives are lived now and that they cannot wait generations for cultural change, many gay and lesbian people themselves are deeply pained by the hurt their sexual identity causes their families and to a lesser extent perhaps their church and community. To know that your parents are disgraced, embarrassed, and shamed by your socially stigmatized sexual identity causes double disgrace, embarrassment, and shame, as well as anger, pity, and potential alienation. Because they love their families, churches, and communities, or would like to, most gay and lesbian people, like heterosexual people who agree with their cause, know the social problem is to keep the faith with what is right while tolerating the compromises of a slow rate of cultural change toward holiness.

How slow? When I was a child growing up in St. Louis, my father tried to explain the racial prejudice that produced segregated water fountains and toilets in public places. When he was growing up, he said, everyone "just knew" that left-handedness was the sign of a deformed character, and in his grade school the left-handed children had their left arm tied down so that they had to use the right hand for writing. In the modern 1940s and 50s of my grammar school education, we knew that to be a false, silly, and harmful prejudice. Many of my classmates and their parents, however, had an equally false, silly, and harmful prejudice about the inferiority of African Americans, or rather about the superiority of white people that was so easily contaminated by intimate contact, as my father put it. He told me that within my lifetime, the racial prejudice that made the sharing of drinking fountains and toilets seem unspeakably gross to my white friends would fall away, and he was right. Were he alive today my father would say that within the lifetime of our college students the prejudice against gay and lesbian people will fall away, not completely, of course, any more than racism is completely gone, but to a very large degree. We see that happening as more people come to know "out" gays and lesbians, especially within their own family and intimate communities. As Christians concerned with the moral right for gays and lesbians on the one hand and for holiness for the whole people of God on the other, we pray that the changes in false cultural assumptions and unjust social arrangements come soon.

But we also pray that the rights and pains of those who are still convinced that homosexuality is sinful, with their personal and communal identity depending on that conviction, genuinely be respected and loved. Only in this way can the church respect the depth of this moral conflict.

While we are waiting for this New Jerusalem to come down out of heaven, however long the wait, we should acknowledge that gay and lesbian people have been forced to live in the church, and elsewhere, as if under a shroud. They have had either to leave the table or to deny they are fully alive as sexual beings. Now is the time to proclaim to them the redeeming word of God. If you will pardon the pun, which I fully intend, John's Jesus "cried with a loud voice, 'Lazarus, come out!' The dead man came out, his hands and feet bound with strips of cloth, and his face wrapped in a cloth. Jesus said to them, 'Unbind him, and let him go.'"

Isaiah said, "On this mountain the Lord of hosts will make for all peoples a feast of rich food, a feast of well-aged wines, of rich food filled with marrow, of well-aged wines strained clear. And he will destroy on this mountain the shroud that is cast over all peoples, the sheet that is spread over all nations; he will swallow up death forever. Then the LORD God will wipe away the tears from all faces, and the disgrace of his people he will take away from all the earth, for the LORD has spoken." Behold, the feast of the Lord. Amen.

23.

ON MARRIAGE

Ruth 3:1-5; 4:13-17
Hebrews 9:24-28
Mark 12:38-44*

BECAUSE OF THE controversies in our country over the legality of gay and lesbian people being able to marry, or being able to have civil or holy unions, it is imperative for responsible preaching to address the issues and not duck them to avoid controversy. I apologize to those who believe it to be unseemly to discuss topics like this from the pulpit, yet I feel obliged to do so because of the deep religious significance and urgency. This sermon concludes an examination of the deep emotional moral conflicts within the church, and also local society, illustrated with discussions of homosexuality.

The wonderful story of Ruth testifies to the profound loyalty that the Moabite woman Ruth had for her Israelite mother-in-law Naomi after the death of her husband, Naomi's son. In our texts, Naomi tells her daughter-in-law to get into bed with Boaz so as to seduce him. Seduced, Boaz then acquires a field that belonged to Naomi, and with the purchase of the field he also acquires Ruth as a wife. The point of the story is that the child Ruth has by Boaz will support Naomi in her old age (and will be the ancestor of King David who is thus not a pure Israelite). Marriage is represented as the commercial transaction of buying a wife motivated by sexual attraction; the function of children is as much support of the elders as carrying on the lineage; and the only love in anything like the modern sense is that between the older and younger women who were in-laws through a previous marriage.

With regard to the legitimacy of contemporary gay and lesbian marriages, we need first to ask about that sense in which marriage is a civil

---

* Lections for Proper 27, Sunday between November 6 and November 12, Year B.

141

union. The civil aspect of marriage does not require love, but it does require a contractual agreement to function in society as a couple. In our society, the marriage contract does not treat women as commercial property. The marriage contract does define such things as tax status, rights to insurance, health benefits, and disposal of estates at death, and the care of and responsibility for children.

Like heterosexual married people, some gay and lesbian people, though by no means all, want to live together as couples, developing the domestic, economic, social, and legal roles of couples. Some political figures who now oppose marriage in the full sense for same-sex couples agree with legalizing civil unions that give such couples the legal benefits of marriage. I see no reason whatsoever not to go along with civil unions in this sense. Viewed strictly as a civil contract, marriage makes a couple with roles of economic and domestic rights and responsibilities. If gay and lesbian people want to enter into such a contract, there is no reason not to allow it. In fact, to disallow it deprives homosexual people of a legal right to enter into certain contracts solely on the basis of their sexual orientation, which is wholly irrelevant to their ability to observe the contracts, to benefit from them, and to contribute to society in the ways that justify civil marriages for heterosexual people.

For most people today, however, marriage means much more than a civil contract, and this colors how they think about the matter of civil unions. Let me attempt to describe this richer reality of marriage in neutral terms. Imagine society, if you will, as composed of a vast ritual dance of interconnecting social roles. I use the phrase "ritual role" in a Confucian sense to mean a general form for interacting with other people and social institutions, like learned stylized steps in a dance. A ritual is a coordination of many such roles in a complicated social dance. A society has rituals within rituals within rituals. Within a society's system of rituals lies a utilitarian core so that the economic, domestic, judicial, military, and other necessary functions are satisfied more or less. Yet the rituals are far richer than their utilitarian functions. They convey the emotional and value-oriented elements of civilized culture, providing both meaning for human life and ordered ways by which human aspirations can be cultivated and satisfied. A society's rituals are dysfunctional when they do not convey the intense satisfactions of civilization, including religious satisfactions.

A ritual role by itself is a kind of abstract form, like the role of being a "student," which means fitting into general patterns of how to spend the day studying, having certain kinds of friends, dressing within the student dress fashions, living around libraries, dormitories, and the like. Each individual has to individuate the social roles in exactly his or her own way. No one is a student in general, only a student in particular, and many different ways exist for individuating student rituals. Personal identity cannot be defined fully in terms of the abstract ritual dances in which one engages, although that is the way we begin to get acquainted—"What do you do? Where do you live? Tell me about your family." Full personal identity is the individuation of those ritual roles with one's own impulses, chemistry, and inward life. In our individuation of social roles we play them more or less well, often very poorly, like D students.

Marriage in our Western society is a very complex ritual dance set among other social rituals. It has all the functional ritual roles outlined in the civil contract of marriage. In addition marriage has at least two more ritual elements. The first has to do with love, something more emphasized in the modern world than in the ancient Hellenistic world. Love begins as children feel themselves loved by parents. With the onset of adolescent hormones, love takes on an intense sexual dimension, and marriage ritual includes being sexual partners as well as friends. Love also extends to the care of others the way the ritual says parents should care for children, with care directed in mutuality between the couple, and perhaps to their extended families, and also to the next generation. The next generation might be blood children or adopted ones or surrogates in a host of other social rituals such as education by which older people care for dependent younger ones. The ritual roles of marriage are intrinsically involved in larger social rituals of care and dependency.

The second ritual element in marriage is that it is a fundamental defining element for personal identity. To be a person as one of a couple is different from being a single person, and this difference can be extremely important, perhaps the most important defining element of identity for many people. The religious importance of personal identity is that it is what we present to God. It is who we are in ultimate perspective.

Remember that I am speaking about the ritual roles, not about their actual individuated performance. In an actual family, one or both of one's biological parents might be missing during the formative years, and whoever functions in the parental roles might be unloving. Love between the partners might be deficient in emotional quality or sexual fulfillment, and people's better friends might be outside the marriage; similarly a couple might be terrible actual parents for their children. One might individuate one's personal identity as a married person as a horrible marriage part-ner—abusive, codependent, emotionally absent, or adulterous. How people individuate the complex of roles that define the ritual character of marriage might be very different from what the rituals themselves call for in terms of ideal performance. Yet I believe that what I have described so briefly is in fact the cultural definition of marriage in contemporary Western society—a definition based on a ritual dance of roles for social functions, love, and personal identity but understood always to be actualized in ways that individuate the roles in better and worse ways. When people talk about the real meaning of marriage, they mean something like this.

The problem with our rancorous debate about homosexuality is that the way we commonly identify such ritual complexes as marriages is with quick images, paradigm cases, or outstanding models. These images are nearly always too one-sided, too selective, to be faithful to the complex social reality. For example, when we think of "captains of industry," the images that come to mind are usually of men, sexists as we are, not of women despite their prominence now in business. With regard to mar-riage, the image, reinforced in literature, art, and tradition for centuries, is of a man and woman married lovingly to each other, each with parents, grandparents, and an extended family, and together having children who in turn will mature and marry. This is the dominant image of marriage in our society. Even when we call to mind the vast complexity of marriage and the distinction between its ritual roles to be performed and the actual performance of them, our thinking of marriage is focused and filtered through the dominant quick image.

Surely those people who claim to be social conservatives are right that few institutions in our society are as important as marriage for purposes of domestic social function, satisfactions of love, and ultimate personal identity. But social conservatives also claim that the heterosexual image of marriage is the only and definitive image of it. They believe that marriage itself, that wonderful ritual complex for human civilization and individual satisfaction, needs to conform to that image.

In point of fact, however, same-sex couples can play all the roles that heterosexual people can in marriage. They can fulfill the contractual eco-nomic and domestic roles, the ritual connections to their own parents and extended family in learning love and care, the rituals of sexual love and fulfillment, the joining of careers and friendship, growing old together, and caring for the next generation, perhaps even in raising children of their own. No reason exists to believe that gay and lesbian people will individuate these roles more or less well than straight couples. There are winning and losing examples of both. I believe that anyone who can bracket out the short-cut images of marriage and think about its complex of ritual roles would agree that people of same-sex desire and commitment can enter faithfully into those ritual roles just the same as people with other-sex desire.

Of course, most people are not going to think of marriage always with the analytical tools of sociology and ritual theory, to which I have appealed here. We usually engage complex social realities by means of our images. Given the facts that about 95 percent of the population here and around the world is heterosexual and that heterosexual marriage is far more efficient than homosexual marriage in matters of procreation, the dominance of heterosexual images of marriage is perfectly understandable. So is the passion with which those images are defended. What is under attack, as understood by people whose sole images of marriage are heterosexual, is not the mere image but the complex institution of marriage itself. Gay and lesbian people make up only about 5 percent of the population, and by no means all of those seek fulfillment in marriage. Very few models or images of same-sex marriages are well-known beyond the gay and lesbian communities. Fueled by very great passion, the resistance to same-sex marriage is a noble defense of the very important social institution of marriage.

But it is misguided, I believe, by its association of the ritual complex of marriage with exclusively heterosexual images. Homosexual images can also be faithful to the complex reality. In time, perhaps not too much time, gay and lesbian couples will be more conspicuous in the community and will be depicted in the media so as to take on iconic functions. For gay and lesbian people to be denied either the legal right to marriage or the social respect of being able to enter into real marriages in the richest sense is unjust. The injustice is based on a confusion of the heterosexual image of marriage with the actual ritual complex of marriage roles that can be played equally well by same-sex couples. Same-sex marriages do indeed threaten the exclusivity of the image of marriage as between a man and a woman. But they do not threaten the reality of heterosexual marriage: they only complement heterosexual ways of individuating the roles of marriage with alternative same-sex ways that are satisfying for people with same-sex desire.

A final point is in order to reflect on the Christian significance of marriage. The Christian gospel is that as God loves us as creatures in our own right, so we should love one another and love God. Jesus taught the ideal of friendship in loving communities as the best context for cultivating love of God and of the others in creation. No evidence exists that he thought of marriage as a particularly good form of loving community, and given the social patterns of dominance and the economic definition of women prevalent in his day, this is understandable. Our own society has developed to the point, however, where marriage, set in the ritual context of family, economy, and cultural life, is a highly prized form of loving community. To be sure it is not for everyone. But for those who seek to find their personal identity as married people, it is perhaps the richest kind of community of love in our culture. Therefore, to deprive gay and lesbian people of the opportunity to enter into marriage and have that blessed by the church is an arbitrary betrayal of the church's mission to foster communities of love.

Let us therefore bless those people who fight for the integrity of marriage in all its complexity, praising God for the passion required to sustain it in a consumer society that would sell it for a profitable mess of pottage. Let us bless those people who recognize that the image of heterosexual marriage depicts only one way of individuating the complex ritual character of marriage, a way fulfilling for those with other-sex desire but devastating for those of same-sex desire. Let us bless those people who provide images of marriage individuated in the multiple ways open to gay and lesbian people and bless those who learn from these new images. Let us bless those who move our social consensus forward with patient but firm conviction to do justice to the gay and lesbian members of our community who are marginalized regarding marriage because our social images are too limited. Let us bless the God who forgives us our mistakes when we remain obdurate in the face of this injustice or when we push so fast as to threaten the social stability within which the precious institution of marriage is meaningful. Let us praise the God who creates from the depths of complexity in the institution of marriage and yet who makes all things new to bring all his children to life. Like Jesus at the wedding at Cana, we revel in joy for life and love. Praise God! Amen.

24.

SHARPER THAN A TWO-EDGED SWORD

Job 23:1-9, 16-17
Hebrews 4:12-16
Mark 10:17-31*

THE TOPIC OF this sermon makes me extremely uncomfortable. I preach about it with reluctance and only because it would be worse to avoid it. The passage from Hebrews states the theme: "Indeed, the word of God is living and active, sharper than any two-edged sword, piercing until it divides soul from spirit, joints from marrow; it is able to judge the thoughts and intentions of the heart. And before him no creature is hidden, but all are naked and laid bare to the eyes of the one to whom we must render an account."

The phrase, "the word of God," has many meanings in Jewish and Christian history. In Genesis, for instance, "the word of the Lord" came to Abraham and Moses, telling them to do something. Throughout the prophetic writings in the Hebrew Bible, "the word of the Lord" is what the prophets hear and then proclaim, and often it is of a critical nature regarding what the people are doing. In the New Testament, the "word of the Lord" or "word of God" is used to describe the gospel, the content of Jesus' preaching. In another sense of the phrase, the Gospel of John begins, "In the beginning was the Word, and the Word was with God, and the Word was God." After saying that the Word is the agent of creation, John goes on to say that the Word became flesh, and this is Jesus.

* Lections for Proper 23, Sunday between October 9 and October 15, Year B.

When the author of the book of Hebrews talks about the Word of God, living and active, sharper than a two-edged sword, he does not mean the high metaphysical notion that John used, nor does he mean it to apply directly to Jesus. Rather he means something like the word of the prophets. Jesus' treatment of the rich man is a case in point, as described in the text from Mark. Matthew's version of the story says the man is young, and Luke's says he is a ruler. The rich young ruler ran up to Jesus as Jesus was setting out on a journey, probably surrounded by his followers. Boasting of neither his wealth nor political power, the young man knelt at Jesus' feet and said, "Good Teacher, what must I do to inherit eternal life?" He seemed a model of earnestness and humility. Jesus, alas, must have been in some kind of negative mood about himself because he snapped at the youth for calling him good, saying that no one is good except God alone. This is odd. The young man probably only meant "Good Teacher" as an honorific title to indicate that he thought Jesus would have good advice; Jesus was rude. On other occasions Jesus claimed great importance for himself and his message, putting a high price on those who would follow him. At any rate, on this occasion Jesus dismissed the appeal for advice, telling the rich young ruler that he already knew the commandments. Jesus listed a few in an offhand manner, probably still distracted by the need to get his entourage under way.

Then something dramatic happened. The young man said quietly that he had kept the commandments from his youth. Jesus looked at him suddenly, probably paying attention for the first time. If the young man had kept the commandments and still came asking how to inherit eternal life, he already knew that keeping the commandments is not enough. The young man knew that Jesus' offhand response to his earnest question was not enough. And Jesus knew that he himself had given a wrong answer: keeping the commandments is not enough. In this way the Word of God came to Jesus, piercing as if to divide his soul from spirit, joints from sinews. He knew that in this instance he had not been a Good Teacher, and he was shocked out of his self-indulgent sulk.

Then what did Jesus do? Looking at the young man, he loved him. Why did he love that young man whom he had just met? Perhaps it was because, even with his wealth and authority, the young man was winsome, humble, and so very earnest about eternal life. Perhaps it was because the man was serious when Jesus had been dismissive. Perhaps it was because the young man unwittingly had become the teacher and Jesus the chastened student. Perhaps it was because Jesus was grateful for the ever-so-humble correction. Perhaps it was because love was simply what Jesus felt toward people to whom he paid serious attention. I think all of these factors were involved.

Looking at the young man with love, Jesus knew immediately what was wrong and what he needed to do. For all his genuine virtue, the young man had identified himself with his wealth and station and needed to give them up. This diagnosis was confirmed in the youth's response, which was to be shocked and to go away grieving. How Jesus must himself have grieved at that response! Jesus was by no means against wealth, and he did not demand that all his friends follow him around. Witness his friendship with Nicodemus, Joseph of Arimathea, and the household of Mary, Martha, and Lazarus. Those people were not in bondage to their wealth. The rich young ruler was. We do not know what happened to him subsequently. Perhaps he did sell his possessions and returned to follow Jesus. Perhaps he lived in denial of his bondage to wealth. Perhaps he knew Jesus was right and simply could not bring himself to act upon the truth. Perhaps in fact he was Joseph of Arimathea and developed a different relation to Jesus without disposing of his possessions. The point is that Jesus' diagnosis and remedy was the Word of God that cut him like a two-edged sword.

That sword hurts, does it not, when it cuts us? Most of us in this are rich in comparison with destitute people in the many hellholes of our planet. Like the young ruler, we have more control over our lives than people do in many places, especially Afghanistan and Iraq, given recent events. The Word of God points out our privilege and also our attachment, our identification with it.

Permit me a side comment here. If you feel guilty about your relative wealth, I have a wonderful suggestion: give generously to the church—practice tithing. The church does good work and needs your support. Contributing to it will do wonders for your guilt. I hope you are awash in guilt about your wealth.

Alas, however, salving guilt is not the same as abandoning attachments, like the rich young man's, to the identity of being wealthy and powerful. What kept the man from eternal life was not his wealth, his authority, his virtue, or even his charity. It was that he let those things define him so that he was in bondage to having them. We too are often in bondage to wealth and power and to many things besides. We need our jobs to give us identity, or our controlling roles in family, or our serving roles in community. Of course jobs are good, the exercise of authority in family nurture is good, and serving others is so good that many people believe it to be the essence of religion. Yet we all know people who pour out their lives in service to others for the sake of being recognized for doing so. We know people who go to church too often to display their piety, who send too many cards of condolence so as to be recognized as sympathetic. We all know people who use virtue for the sake of gaining importance in the eyes of others and in their own eyes, not for its own sake. We might be people who do that. Service should be invisible; piety should be inconspicuous, seen only by God; sympathy should be genuine and spontaneous. Charity should be for the sake of the need, not for the appearance of generosity. The Word of God cuts especially sharply into the bones and sinews of good people, church people, the people who would run up to Jesus, kneel at his feet, and ask how to obtain eternal life.

The reason for the pain of the two-edged sword is that it makes us see ourselves suddenly in God's ultimate perspective. The Word of God tells us that how we appear to others does not matter ultimately. The Word of God tells us that the fables we rehearse about ourselves to bolster our egos, about our virtues and our vices, about our successes and also about our troubles, do not matter ultimately. What matters is what we do and who we are in God's eyes. If we possess wealth and exercise power for the sake of status rather than because of the good they can do, we cannot accept God's perspective until the Word of God cuts the bondage of attachment. If we perfect virtue and practice generous charity for the sake of the recognition it brings rather than their intrinsic worth, we cannot accept God's perspective until the Word of God cuts the bondage of attachment. By all means, be economically productive and exercise responsible leadership. Perfect the virtues of humane living and don't forget the needs of your congregation. But we should not be bound by these good things any more than we should be bound by sin. The sharp Word of God is not only for the evil-doers and sinners, for the despairing and lost. It is for winsome people like the rich young ruler. And ourselves.

Jesus' remedy for the rich young man was to ask him to become a follower and to free himself up so that he could do that. The young man recognized his bondage when he realized how much it hurt to give himself to God, and he grieved. As your preacher, I ask you to give yourself to God. We already belong to the Creator and giving ourselves to God merely acknowledges that truth. That truth strips us naked of self-serving pretenses, but naked is how we come into the world and how we will leave. Does something hold you back? It might not be money or power; it might not be a need for reputation or anything I can imagine. You will know it when you hesitate. If you don't understand it, you can find help in discernment, perhaps a lifelong process.

I don't know what giving yourself to God means in your case. It might mean becoming morally serious for the first time, or truly committing yourself to your relationships, or abandoning a false patriotism, or finding more socially useful work, or giving up on feeling sorry for yourself. You can tell when you have given yourself to God because you love God's creatures for just what they are, not for what they pretend to be or for what they do for your benefit. You take joy in praising God for the glories of creation and also for the troubles of your life, knowing that had the rich young man followed Jesus he would have arrived at the cross, not at social or political victory.

The rich young man knew right where to come to find the Word of God for himself. God has graced the world with countless witnesses to the word. But the young man turned away from it and grieved his own bondage. Isn't that our trouble too? When Jesus and his disciples discussed the young man later, Jesus said it is almost impossible for the rich to shed the baggage that keeps them from God. But then, he said, with God all things are possible. So I invite you to the throne of grace. Please leave behind your wealth and also your poverty. Leave your power and also your victimization. Leave your virtues and also your vices. Leave your good fortune and also your troubles. Leave your pleasures and also your suffering. Leave your successes and also your failures. Pray without baggage for a Word of God that lets you see yourself as God sees you, however sharply that sword bites.

Jesus looked at the rich young man and loved him. That is God's regard for us. Can we accept that love which, like a two-edged sword, severs the truth about us from the pretenses to which we are bound? With God, all things are possible. Amen.

SACRAMENT

25

BAPTISM OF THE HOLY SPIRIT

Isaiah 43:1-7
Acts 8:14-17
*Luke 3:15-17, 21-22**

ODAY IS THE first Sunday after Epiphany in the church calendar, and it celebrates Jesus' baptism when, according to Luke, he was blessed by the Holy Spirit and the voice from heaven said to him, "You are my Son, the Beloved; with you I am well pleased." My own baptism was not half so spectacular, I can tell you. I was nine and remember vividly going to the chancel rail with my parents in the Methodist Church in St. Louis where I grew up. The minister was saying words I didn't understand, and when he dipped his hand in the bowl of water and pressed it down on my head, the brittle hair fixer my mother had slathered on my unruly mop shattered and crackled with a most upsetting sensation of something breaking. That was not an epiphany, although I wish I still had the hair.

The text from Luke actually makes reference to three baptisms. First, John the Baptist was conducting a revival with mass baptisms for repentance and cleansing from sin. Second, Jesus, who came to John for that Baptism, was uniquely revealed by the Spirit and Word to be the Son of God. And third, although first in our text, John says that Jesus himself will bring a baptism not of water but of Spirit and fire. These three different references to baptism all have significant meanings as they have been

---

* Lections for the First Sunday after the Epiphany, Year C.

developed within the Christian tradition. Christian baptism, of course, is not literally any of these, except perhaps the last; rather it is the ceremony of initiation into the Christian life, into membership in the church. I believe that we need a new awakening of the meaning of our baptism, not that those who have been baptized need to be baptized again but that we need to catch the Spirit and fire of what it has meant all along.

The first meaning of baptism is obvious from the symbolism, namely a washing away of our sins. Sin is symbolized as dirt, uncleanness. Many Christians, especially those called "Baptists" (not unexpectedly), believe that a person needs to be totally immersed. Like John the Baptist who called upon people to repent of their sins and baptized them in the Jordan only after they had repented as a symbolic act of making them clean, many Baptists and others today believe that only people old enough to understand what they are doing and genuinely repent should be baptized, a custom called "believer's baptism."

Other Christians, however, note that the cleansing from sin is an act of God and not a reward for repentance. So they baptize infants who are presented by their parents. Whatever kind of original sin a baby might have inherited, and there are many conflicting beliefs about that, it is washed away with the ritual, and the child is incorporated as a full member of the Christian community. The parents, godparents, and the whole household of God are charged with the education of the child in Christian piety. Whether of infants, nine year olds, or hardened repentant sinners, baptism means that the baptized people ever after are members of the Christian church, for whom other Christians have a responsibility, regardless of whether they carry on congregational membership, moral seriousness, or Christian belief. No one ever needs to be baptized twice.

Let me tell you then that if you have been baptized, and yet you feel burdened by guilt, that burden is unnecessary. You might well be guilty and something should be done about that. But you should not be burdened by the guilt or let it keep you from God. The author of Colossians wrote, "And when you were dead in trespasses … God made you alive together with him, when he forgave us all our trespasses, erasing the record that stood against us with its legal demands. He set this aside, nailing it to the cross" (Col. 2:13-14). Remember the verse from Horatio Spafford's 1873 hymn, "It is Well with My Soul": "My sin, oh, the bliss of this glorious thought! My sin, not in part but the whole, is nailed to the cross, and I bear it no more, praise the Lord, praise the Lord, O my soul." If you feel such a burden, then take your baptism seriously, renew the baptismal vows that you made or that were made for you at your baptism and participate in the full grace of the Christian community. If you have not been baptized, enter into the process of becoming so.

The second sense of baptism is deeper in meaning, if such a thing is possible. In this sense, baptism is going down with Jesus into the waters of death and then rising from those waters in resurrection. The author of Colossians wrote to the people of that congregation, "When you were buried with him in baptism, you were also raised with him through the faith in the power of God, who raised him from the dead" (Col. 2:12). When John the Baptist put Jesus under the waters of the Jordan, like returning to the primeval chaos before creation, he prefigured Jesus' death. When Jesus rose from the waters and the Holy Spirit descended, like the divine wind in the beginning, this prefigured Jesus' resurrection. When we Christians are baptized, we die with Jesus to the old life of sin and rise with Jesus to the new life, the new creation, in which we are already embraced eternally with God. The author of Colossians went on to say, "So if you have been raised with Christ, seek the things that are above, where Christ is, seated at the right hand of God. Set your minds on things that are above, not on things that are on earth, for you have died, and your life is hidden with Christ in God" (Col. 3:1-3). I pray that you have a musical ear for these wonderful symbols of the Christian faith.

Of course the resurrection of life in baptism, enjoyed by all Christians, does not mean the end of daily life and its problems. The author of Colossians goes on to say that resurrected Christians should put to death the old patterns of sin and put on the new ways of God: "But now you must get rid of all such things—anger, wrath, malice, slander, and abusive language from your mouth. Do not lie to one another, seeing that you have stripped off the old self with its practices and have clothed yourselves with the new self, which is being renewed in knowledge according to the image of its creator. In that renewal there is no longer Greek and Jew, circumcised and uncircumcised, barbarian, Scythian, slave and free; but Christ is all and in all!" (Col. 3:8-11). As baptized Christians, dead to sin and raised to new life in Christ, we don't have to worry about sin's burdens or the fear of death. Our only concerns now are sanctification and holiness. We have the Holy Spirit, God's creative power present throughout all creation, to discipline and guide us.

The third meaning of baptism follows precisely from this. John the Baptist said Jesus would baptize not with water but with the Holy Spirit and fire. I suspect from other things he said that John thought that Jesus would be an even fiercer judge than he himself had been. But the subsequent Christian understanding of Jesus' baptism in the Holy Spirit is more complicated than moral judgment. It means at least four things, I believe.

First, baptism in the Holy Spirit means that God is with us in the process of sanctification in which we put aside our old bad habits one by one and take up the habits of new life, as described in the last Colossians passage. What does this mean in practice? It means that the creative power of God is all around us, in the renewing powers of nature, in our bodies' natural healing processes, in the natural desire of people to help, and in our own love of life. Many things hold us back, especially feelings of guilty unworthiness. But we have died to those things and are free for God's renewing power to run through us like a river.

Second, baptism in the Holy Spirit is in all the things of religion, especially the church, which provides patterns of good life, symbols to connect us with redeeming powers, congregations of people with whom life builds up all who participate, scriptures to read, theology to contemplate, service to render others, songs to sing, dances to dance, and messages to preach to witness the Spirit in our lives. What does this mean in practice? It means we need constantly to be alert to the discernment of the true Holy Spirit in contrast to the tempting spirits of evil, for we all know that religion can be harmful, that the church sometimes advocates destructive patterns of life, that symbols can be used demonically, that congregations can be dysfunctional, that theologies can lie, that service can be manipulative, that songs can destroy the spirit, that dances can become marches, and that testimony can preach hate. The Christian life collectively and individually is a constant critical discernment of spirits, measuring their claims by the fruits of the Holy Spirit. With our own spirits alert, the Holy Spirit can be discerned in the incredibly rich resources of the Body of Christ such that our new lives have powers to heal the world as well as ourselves.

Third, the indwelling of the Holy Spirit in which Christ baptizes us manifests the love of God toward us, patient, kind, and lovely. When Jesus was baptized, the divine voice called him "My Son, my beloved," and as we are grafted onto Christ as branches of the true vine, we become aware of being beloved children of God. This is celebrated in our public worship. In the ancient church the communal enjoyment of the blessings of God's love in the Holy Spirit was expressed sometimes through ecstatic speaking in tongues, and many Christian congregations experience that today. Even more, God's love can be felt in the depths of our hearts as our spiritual discipline teaches us to be silent and still. The life of prayer, meditation, and contemplation in private, often guided by a spiritual director, can lead to profound experiences of God's loving, correcting, comforting spiritual vitality. As Augustine said, when you go deep enough within your own soul you find not yourself but God. Divine ecstasy means being "beside yourself," which can take place in charismatic worship as well as in profound contemplation.

The fourth meaning of Christ's baptism with the Holy Spirit and fire is the genuine ecstasy of turning from glorying in God's love for us to our loving God as our beloved. If we are truly created in God's image, and God is the great lover who creates the world and redeems creation, then it is not enough for us to receive God's love. We fulfill God's image by loving as God loves. We can love the Creator in all things created, for which the shorthand expression is loving our neighbors. And we can love the Creator God as our beloved. Loving God is not exactly like loving another being, because God is the depths of our own hearts, the ground of our being. But loving God is not loving only the God in us. Through the Holy Spirit, which is God in us, we can love the Creator of the entire cosmos. This is not easy, because that Creator gives us suffering and death as well as all the graces of life. Probably we have to hate God before we can love God seriously. When we do take God as our lover, our beloved, our own sense of self sinks to insignificance. The fire of sexual ecstasy has long been the best symbol for the ecstasy of loving God. When the Holy Spirit brings us to love God, who can say whether it is we giving ourselves to God in the Spirit loving us, or we in the Spirit loving God, or God loving God in us, or we loving the creation in God? Please groan in the Spirit to be God's lover, for it is part of baptism in the Holy Spirit and fire (Rom. 8:22-25).

I have represented these four meanings of being baptized in the Holy Spirit and fire as if they were separate, yet they are intimately connected and grow into one another. Personal sanctification, communal holiness, personal and communal experience of God's love, and the ecstasy of loving God are integral parts of the one fire of Christian life. The light that came into the world in Christ brings our misdeeds to life and cleanses them. It leads us through the death of our old selves to new lives of holiness. It sets us aglow with the power of sanctification, communal holiness, the experience of God's love, and the ecstasy of loving God. In that light, we can turn from our self-concerns and live for others as free friends and lovers of God. The appearance of Jesus makes all this possible.

If you are a Christian whose sense of your baptism has fallen asleep, I invite you to wake up. Do you long for cleansing from sin, for going through death to true life, for sanctification, holy community, the knowledge of God's love for you, and the ecstasy of loving God? Then become a Christian in a serious way. It's time for a Great Awakening of the Holy Spirit in us and in our land. Do not settle for being what John Wesley called an "almost Christian." Like Jesus, come to the baptism of the Holy Spirit. Amen.

26.

WHO COMES TO THE TABLE? (A COMMUNION SERMON)

Job 1:1; 2:1-10
Hebrews 1:1-4; 2:5-12
*Mark 10:2-16**

I GREW UP in a Midwestern Methodist Church that celebrated the Lord's Supper because it had to and only because of that. The Methodist rules in those days said each congregation had to serve Communion once a quarter and most of the people in my church thought that was much too often. A great many stayed home on Communion Sundays because the service was too long, running over into the Sunday dinner hour. My parents used the excuse that my brother and I would fidget too much if we tried to sit through the service. Perhaps this was after he and I poured grape juice on each other from those little cups that were in vogue then.

The Eucharist, along with baptism, is a nearly universal sign of the unity of the Christian movement, despite the diversity in how it is done. Christians of all kinds have celebrated some form of the Lord's Supper in every culture since the beginning. One exception I know is the Salvation Army, which does not use that rite but considers every member to be part of the communion loaf. Some Christian communities celebrate the Eucharist daily, others weekly, monthly, or quarterly. The forms of the liturgy have varied greatly, as well as the languages used. The theologies

---

* Lections for Proper 22, Sunday between October 2 and October 8, Year B.

explaining the Eucharist have also varied and often been at odds with one another. Some Roman Catholics believe the elements are changed into the very blood and body of Jesus; some Protestants believe the service is just a memorial; some Orthodox believe it is an enactment of heaven; and there are many positions in between. In point of fact, the Eucharist is a symbolic act with many meanings all interwoven. To single out any one as theologians like to do nearly always results in a distorted abstraction. Whatever our theologies, nearly all those meanings are operative in the souls of individuals and communities when they come to the Eucharistic table.

The placing of the table itself has variable theological significance. More common among Roman Catholics and Anglicans than liturgically free Protestants is the practice of putting the table against the wall at the back of the choir. The presider at the Eucharist, that is, the minister or priest in charge, turns his or her back on the congregation to face the table, usually called an altar, and enacts the sacrifice of handling the symbols of Jesus' body and blood. The theological significance of this is that the presider leads the people to God and reaches up at the moment of consecration. God descends to meet the people in the consecrated elements. The wisdom in this way of performing the Eucharist is that it breaks the congregation's sense that it is whole and complete in itself. No matter how harmonious, no congregation is complete in itself. No matter how cozy we are with the confidence that God is in our midst, we should know that God is wild, not a tame lion as C. S. Lewis warned in his Narnia books. We need to reach up beyond our boundaries to hope that God comes. And when God comes, that is a mystery breaking in upon us that is not entirely predictable, not entirely contained in the consumption of bread and wine, and not entirely safe. That's the good part of the Eucharistic practice of leading the people to God. The difficulty felt with this form of the Eucharist is that it seems to make the presider too special a person, a mediator, who in fact separates the people from God. The presider, a priest or minister, is a specially trained and accredited representative of the people, but only one of the people, not someone holier than the people.

The more common Eucharistic form now is to move the altar forward and call it Christ's table with the presider and helpers behind it, beckoning the congregation to come sit at the table as at a dinner party, or at least as close as can be arranged in a large group. This form runs the risk of domesticating God as a foodstuff in our midst. The Lord's Supper is not merely a gathering of pals to remember good old Jesus. The virtue of this form, however, is that it symbolically establishes the context of the

Eucharist as Christ's table. Jesus' dinners were the context in which he taught, learned, and practiced the love among friends that was his ideal and lesson. We are invited to go to dinner with Jesus, and though you might think rightly that we ministers have been a sorry lot of substitute hosts these last two thousand years, this still is Jesus' table.

His table was no ordinary one and was never entirely domesticated. Like God breaking in upon a worshiping community, Jesus broke boundaries with his dinners. He ate with friends, but also with strangers. He brought tax abusers and prostitutes to his table. He ate with rich people and poor people. He ate with strange women, which Jewish men were not supposed to do. He healed Peter's mother of sickness so she could cook his dinner. He ate with at least one man he had brought back from death to life. A woman washed his feet with tears, dried them with her hair at the table, and poured embalming perfume on him. The crumbs under his table healed people. He washed his disciples' feet before dinner. It was at the table that he asked to be remembered in the form of his bloody death, with bread as his broken body and wine as his spilled blood. At the table, the last night, as the Beloved Disciple lay against him, he told his friends that the community of love they had formed was what his whole work was about, that it was made possible because of God's love, which he had taught them, that this community of love would sustain them through troubles and persecutions, and that they should extend the circle of loving friendships around the world. It was at the table that Jesus said goodbye to his friends, knowing they would betray, deny, or desert him. Jesus' table broke all the rules about who could eat together and what table fellowship means. God was at his table making all things new.

So we are all invited now to Jesus' table. Some Christians believe that special requirements of confession and good faith with God must be met before coming to the table; our ritual has a confession, absolution, and a passing of the peace to symbolize a renewed people. But we do not require that you be right with God before you come. Jesus did not do that at his table. Some Christians insist that participants be baptized members of the community before being allowed to receive Communion, and that is a conventional assumption. But Jesus had no such strictures for his dinners. Following John Wesley, the Methodist founder, who taught that the Eucharist is a means of grace, not only a privilege of membership, we say that Jesus' table is open and invite you all.

If you feel guilty for sexual thoughts and misdeeds, there is an honored biblical place for you at this table. If you cheat and exploit others in business, crooked tax collectors were at the table before you. If you are an outsider, unused to our ways, remember the strange diversity of Jesus' crowd for which he was criticized. If you are a devoted friend of Jesus, lean on him here. If you think Jesus has some good reason to judge you harshly, know that instead he invites you to dinner, leaving you free to mend your ways or not. If you feel uncomfortable with all these unlikely people Jesus has brought to the table with you, you need to laugh at your own discomfort when Jesus breaks the rules. This is not a domestic table. This is the table of a new world. God comes to this table. Come lean on him and know that you are touching something holy. Amen.

27

BELIEF, WORKS, CULT
(A COMMUNION SERMON)

Romans 13:11-14
James 2:14-17*
Mark 7:24-37*

I N WHAT SENSES are you religious? The modern world usually identifies religion with belief on the one hand and religiously defined good
works on the other. When you ask what people's religion is, most often
you do so by asking about their religious beliefs. When you are in crisis
about your own religion, most often it is because you doubt what you
think you are supposed to believe.

However, we all know people of deep piety whose belief system is embar-
rassingly simple-minded and confused. For most of us, our grandparents
were like that, and, for many of us, we ourselves were like that only months
ago. Yet we know that the sincerity of such simple-minded faith frequently
characterizes saints who are self-sacrificing, deeply attentive to the needs of
others, committed to steady support of family, unflagging in work, loyal to
friends, and filled with joy, hope, peace, and love. Paul said these virtues are
marks of the Holy Spirit. Most of us, in practice, follow the author of The
Letter of James in the pragmatic definition of the religious life: it's what you
do that counts. That also is the clue to what you really believe deep down,
below the level of conscious thought and choice. So two ways are commonly used to think about being religious: belief and good works.

A third way to identify a person's religion, however, is by looking at that
person's cult. "Cult" is a word with bad connotations for some people for
whom it refers to a radical sect that steals people away from their home

---

*Lections for Proper 18 between September 4 and September 10, Year B.

culture and brainwashes them into a new and narrow culture. The basic meaning of the word, however, is simply education, the taking on of a culture or way of life by practicing its elements. We "cultivate" the educated life in the university by practices such as lectures and classes, research and study, use of the library and laboratory, coffee breaks and informal discussions, artistic productions and athletic fanaticism, all-night arguments and exam-cramming, attending conferences, writing grant proposals, publishing papers, celebrating academic successes, especially in relation to Harvard, and telling congratulatory stories about what good teachers, students, and staff members we are. Individually, these practices have their pragmatic purposes. Collectively, they are rituals that inculturate us into the deep patterns of critical academic life. As we follow those practices as rituals, they come to pattern our habitual behavior and thought.

So it is with religion. People who have no practiced pattern of life for relating to ultimate matters have disorganized religion, or no religion, even if they have religious beliefs and do good works associated with religious people. Those people stumble on ultimate matters of life and death haphazardly, unprepared on the deep levels of habitual behavior and thought.

Saint Augustine, who lived in the late fourth and early fifth centuries, was one of the greatest of all Christian theologians. The drama of his autobiography, which he called his *Confessions*, centered on his conversion to Christianity. Raised by a pious Christian mother, he had strayed to other religions and distinctly non-Christian practices. He struggled with the intellectual content of Christian belief relative to other beliefs and could find no decisive argument. He also struggled with whether to give up his licentious but enjoyable life. The crisis came to a head one day when he and a friend were in a garden anguishing over whether to convert to Christianity. Augustine heard some children on the other side of the wall singing, "Take and read, take and read." He picked up a Bible that was open to Romans 13:14 where Paul said to "put on the Lord Jesus Christ." The theologian Carl Vaught has shown that the Latin words were those used for a young man putting on the robe that marked manhood and citizenship.[1] Augustine took that to mean that he should put on the clothing of a Christian, as it were, to vest himself in the Christian way of life, and to enter into the cultic practice of Christianity.

---

1. See Carl G. Vaught, "Theft and Conversion: Two Augustinian Confessions," in *The Recovery of Philosophy in America: Essays in Honor of John Edwin Smith,* Thomas P. Kasulis and Robert Cummings Neville, eds. (Albany: State University of New York Press, 1997), especially p. 241.

What did that mean for him? It meant taking up the Christian practices of worship and prayer, leaving his friends who could not tolerate that, and befriending Christians and those who were supportive of his vesting himself in the Christian cult. It meant reading the Bible, participating in the rituals of the church through the liturgical calendar, and observing the sacraments of the church. In quick time, Augustine was ordained a priest and then a bishop. For decades, he administered a diocese in Hippo in North Africa and was one of the most prolific theological writers of all times in any religion.

He "put on" the Christian way and, clothed in the Christian cult, worked out the belief contents of his faith. Augustine was one of the most rigorous, critical, questioning, and creative thinkers ever, and his theology is a root inheritance of Western Christianity, Roman Catholic and Protestant. He never pretended to believe something he really doubted. But his theology was worked out within the context of the cultic practice of Christian life. The cultic practice of Christianity gave him the freedom to question, doubt, and explore beyond the then boundaries of Christian belief.

The cultic practice most common to Christians around the world and from the beginning is the Eucharist, which we are about to celebrate. The form of its celebration varies, and we shall follow a liturgy derived from the United Methodist tradition. Participating in the Eucharistic liturgy shapes the soul, no matter what you might be thinking about on a conscious level. Repeated participation is a bones-and-muscle education in the deep grammar of Christian life. We have no rules here about who can take Communion, not even that you have to be baptized, only that you should understand it to be a way of putting on the Christian life like a garment marking emerging maturity and citizenship in the church.

The Eucharist is a liturgical rite with many layers of intertwined meanings, resonating together to shape the cultivation of Christian character and community. First and foremost it combines symbols of death—Jesus' spilt blood and broken body—with symbols of renewed life—the elements are food for life. Crucifixion and resurrection go together in many senses for Christian vision and practice. Second, the Eucharist symbolizes the universal table of Christians all over the world, even those whose civilizations are incomprehensible to us and whose nations are our enemies: more important than our differences is that we have all put on Christ and eat at his table. The Eucharist has many other levels of meaning, but perhaps the most disturbing is that it is a symbolic cannibal ritual in which we eat the symbols of Jesus' flesh and blood. What could be so serious in life that we are drawn to consume symbolic flesh and blood? Know for now that you have no more serious business with God than what is addressed symbolically by participation in the Eucharistic celebration. The Eucharist in the Christian cult is practice at being right with God.

So today I invite you to the table. Come, you who are saints, to this cultic part of the Christian life that deepens your character and community: you shouldn't miss this opportunity. Come, you who are Christian by mere custom and social arrangement: here your Christianity becomes more serious. Come, you who have fallen away from Christian practice because of boredom or because of disagreement concerning belief or the direction of moral efforts or because of guilt at moral failings: with this act you put on the Christian way again, and all the exciting power of thought and action are yours anew in freedom. Come, you who are considering the Christian way: try on our clothes and see how they feel. Come, you who are confused, self-hating, angry, despairing, fearful, lonely, loveless, or lost: come to this table and for at least a moment put on a way of life that promises direction, forgiveness, joy, hope, courage, companionship, love, and a home in God.

We celebrants are not personally worthy to offer you these elements, and so we dress in liturgical disguises, vestments of the Christian cult. You, beloved, can come as you are. Amen.